*By
the Editors
of Sunset Books
and
Sunset Magazine*

Decorating
with
Plants

Lane Publishing Co., Menlo Park, California

Acknowledgments

In preparing *Decorating with Plants*, we have received the cooperation and help of numerous home owners, horticulturists, interior designers, and architects. We are very grateful to all of them. In particular, our thanks go to these specialists from the plant world: Maggie Baylis, Dorothy Knecht, Baruch Himmilstein, Carol Senter, Nancy Hewitt, Molbak's Nursery, and Baker and Chantry. For their ideas on incorporating plants into the home, we are grateful to interior designers Esther Reilly and William Gaylord.

Edited by Denise Van Lear

Research Editors: Kathryn L. Arthurs
Alyson S. Gonsalves
Lynne B. Morrall

Design: Joe di Chiarro

Illustrations: Carole Etow

Cover: Blooming basketful of elegant phalaenopsis orchid (moth orchid), hydrangea flower clusters, and low-growing *Rhipsalidopsis gaertneri* (Easter cactus) creates a springtime tabletop accent in this decorative plant scheme by Fioridella. A thin layer of sphagnum moss helps hide the flower pots. *Schefflera actinophylla* (Queensland umbrella, octopus tree) provides a green backdrop. Cover design: Zan Fox. Photograph: Jack McDowell.

Editor, Sunset Books: David E. Clark

Second Printing August 1981

 Library of Congress No. 81-82267. ISBN 0-376-03342-8. Lithographed in the United States.

Contents

Magical multiplication
*Maximize the beauty of that one special
Dendrobium phalaenopsis. Surround it
with mirrors that reflect and expand its
blooms into a visual bouquet.*

At Home with Plants

Elegance *au naturel*
Like enormous green hands, the leaves of
Philodendron selloum *and* Philodendron eichleri *create canopies in a monochromatic room. From the straw carpet
and wicker furniture to the cedar trunk
tables, the room has both natural warmth
and elegance. On the mantel are young
palms, and three Aechmeas (bromeliads)
decorate the table tops. Design: Michael
Taylor.*

Decorating with potted plants is not so recent a phenomenon as one might think. The tradition of weaving plants into the home environment dates back as many as 5,000 years to a time when the Chinese created indoor gardens with beautifully cultivated shrubs and flowers, many of which were given special status in their own ornate earthenware containers.

Archeological evidence points to the possibility that Greek and Roman gardeners achieved some success in creating an indoor environment suited to growing various plants throughout the year. Documented attempts in the 17th century include the *orangeries* built in France to produce orange and other citrus plants for royalty.

The Victorians developed elaborate structures that provided the perfect climate for growing the many exotic plant specimens that were zealously collected from all parts of the British Empire. Curiously, these new improved greenhouses were rarely used for growing food crops, and many of the plants found their way into Victorian parlors.

By the early 1970s, the endlessly waxing and waning interest in house plants had grown to enormous proportions. In 1975, over 500 million such plants were sold in the United States alone. Often plant buyers were indiscriminate, buying anything and everything . . . "I can't remember its name, but they said it was easy to grow."

Such chaotic collecting has lately been super-seded by a truer delight in plants, not only as in-dividual objects of beauty but also as contributors to the total indoor environment. Plants are evaluated in terms of how they relate to furniture, room dimensions, color, and mood. Even the tex-ture of leaves and the forms of branches are con-sidered decorative elements. Where the plant sits in relation to its neighbors is important. Plants with color, plants with bloom, are winning new interest, and even orchids are no longer the pet of the privileged few.

Plants bring richness and change. They are ex-tensions of a once very accessible but now often unattainable great outdoors. Plants translate an environment for eating, sleeping, and relaxing into an oasis where tensions and boredom are

Just ducky
A basketful of Lindernia grandiflora (blue angel tears) in a guest bathroom makes a whimsical sink companion. With good light this charming little plant has no difficulty blooming indoors. Design: Rela Gleason.

Kitchen companions
All through this bright white room, plants coexist with busy kitchen activity. High above the vintage gas range are Aechmea fasciata (bromeliads) in a wicker basket; just below it is a Chlorophytum comosum (spider plant). On the counter two luscious azaleas share a wire utility basket, and an array of herbs—chives, catnip, parsley, oregano, and basil—gather in a bright red pebble-filled tray. The rectangular wicker basket brims with Hedera helix (English ivy). Design: Robert C. Peterson.

..At Home with Plants

dispelled. They can be playful. They add style. They can lead the eye, stop the eye, and define space.

There are no hard rules for the relationships between plants and people, no dictums on how to live more pleasantly with plants. No grandiose opinions of art, no computer charts point the way. No one else lives quite the way you live or has your own awareness of convenience, of privacy, of beauty, of daring. Still, what someone else has tried may just give you an idea to adapt to your own life style.

That's why the information in this book will be important to you . . . to guide and direct you in the myriad wonderful ways you can incorporate plants into your home. In addition to the decorating ideas on pages 12–63, you'll find "Basic Plant Care" (pages 64–73) and the "Plant Selection Guide" (pages 74–79), sections that will assist you in assuring your plants a long and healthy life. Chances are if you've made a habitat that suits your way of life, you'll enjoy giving your plants the same consideration. And if they have a stable home in your home, the pleasures you'll glean from decorating with plants will be manifold.

Your own decorating style

Today you can draw on any ethnic, historic, or contemporary style of decorating. No single school limits your choices: you can mix oriental with early American, natural wood with glass and metal, bentwood chairs with African primitives. But whatever your taste in decorating, it will to some degree affect the types of plants you choose for your home.

Some plants just naturally suit some life styles. Does your environment say "I want repose"? Is your room casual, romantic, quiet, with a comfortable sofa, fireplace, a sense of closeness that you like? Then stay away from the rigid plants —the fiddleleaf fig, the yucca, or the cactus. In-

As early as 5,000 years ago, *the Chinese cultivated flowers and shrubs indoors in earthenware containers.*

stead, reach for a handsome queen palm (see page 37) or several large pots of white-blooming spathiphyllum (page 39). Gather flowering plants near the windows . . . cyclamen, begonias, or brightly colored geraniums.

Do you prefer sleekness, chrome, lots of light, brilliant color? Rooms with these features have clarity, sharpness, no mystery. The sculptural form of a dracaena (page 61), the fountain shapes of bromeliads (page 6), the starkness of the pencil tree (page 48), and the bold and shapely euphorbia (page 60)—these perform best with bright, light decors.

Against the dark woods of Mediterranean furniture, elegant tropical-looking plants and smaller ferns work magic. Scandinavian interiors generally have a "designed" look, and delicate vining plants can lighten the setting. Country-style decorating that uses simple antique furniture and old oriental carpets likes "country" greenery —geraniums and begonias on the window sill, hanging baskets of Swedish ivy and spider plants overhead.

(Continued on next page)

...At Home with Plants

Ferns, palms, and orchids have an authentic Victorian heritage, while spathiphyllum and cymbidium are compatible with the art deco look. With 17th and 18th century furnishings, urned ivies elegantly pruned to topiary forms, and ferns set atop pedestals emphasize an overall formal appearance. And if you lean toward the eclectic, the whole world of house plants is at your happy disposal.

Design basics

Plants are among the least expensive and most effective accessories you can purchase. And don't overlook plants as furniture, too. In either role, wisely placed, they can work magic, creating exactly the effect you want for your room and preventing it from appearing over or underdecorated, over or underfurnished.

For an exercise in types and placement of plants, find some pictures in this book showing decorating styles that reflect your taste. Then put your finger tips over the plants in the pictures, and you'll see that, though attractively decorated, the settings will seem bare without the lively presence of plants.

This is where you can put your green thinking to work. Visualize the spaces in your home that need filling in and softening, and the types of foliage that would best do the job. If you plan to use a lot of plants in your room, try grouping them, much as you would furniture. Too many plants spread singly around a room can be confusing to the eye and completely lacking in emphasis. And, too great a mixture of species in a group can also be confusing. A really effective way of grouping plants is by plant types —consider a small forest of attractively grouped palms, for instance.

Plants are natural companions for such table top accessories as lamps, pictures, decorative bowls, and figurines. And as table centerpieces, they can turn a simple meal into an esthetic experience.

Plants live well in the odd spaces, if you can provide for their light needs. The stair landing, the entrance hall, the gap behind the TV, the space in front of a stationary glass door to patio or deck, a bare-bones balcony, a skylighted hall, a dressing room corner, a basement with light and warmth, a study bookcase—all of these are likely places for plants.

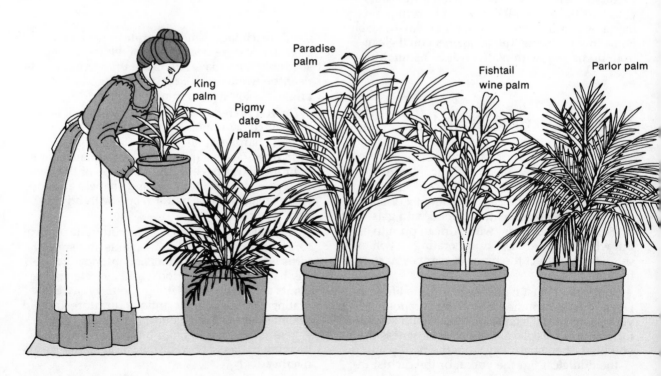

King palm

Pigmy date palm

Paradise palm

Fishtail wine palm

Parlor palm

A sense of scale

The word *scale* has a number of meanings, but the particular definition that applies here is the one architects refer to — the relationship of one object to another. The scale, or size, of a room, of the furniture, of yourself, of windows and doors, and how everything fits together is most important in the selection of any plants you bring in.

Big rooms demand big thinking: plan to have at least one tall tree or several good-size plants at different heights and grouped together (see page 61). One Chinese fountain palm, with its 3-foot leaves, can bring more impact into space than if you spent many times its cost on a new sofa. Place the palm in a giant bamboo basket and instantly the spaces in the room take on new relationships (see page 39).

High ceilings call for at least one spreading tree-size beauty to minimize the height scale. Tall, thin plants, on the other hand, help give the appearance of height to rooms with too-low ceilings. In short, the right plant for the right spot can literally make a problem of scale in a room disappear.

When you see a plant in a nursery that you absolutely must have, remember that it won't look quite the same in your room. The reason is that in the nursery, all the spaces around the plant, and all the other foliage sizes nearby, can fool your eye. So if you have a place in mind where you want to change the feeling or the scale of a room, measure it before you shop. Then, for happy matchmaking, measure the plant (in all its dimensions) as well as the container.

Altering appearances

There are always a few flaws that furniture and lighting cannot solve . . . built-in mistakes like awkwardly located windows, too many doors, outlets that are eyesores, doorways that funnel traffic right through the middle of a conversation group. Nothing seems to resolve the dilemma—nothing, that is, until you take the green way out.

Plants can fool the eye in the nicest ways, emphasizing positive pleasure and stopping the eye from looking at what is behind the greenery. A large Norfolk Island pine, for instance, will close off an unnecessary door. A cymbidium orchid on a pedestal can hide an outlet or a speaker, or even a water mark on the wallpaper; and it can certainly dress up a drab corner.

Vines like grape ivy can be trained to climb a simple piece of burlap hung to cover a cracked wall, drawing delicate patterns of intense beauty. An espaliered fig tree or a portable wooden screen laden with asparagus ferns can divide a room that is long and narrow. And an airy *Ficus benjamina* or coffee tree can relax the symmetry of a room that is dull and formal and too neatly balanced.

When you let plants soften, define, cover, create ambience, or hint at mystery, your slightly off-kilter room or ugly duckling space can turn into a welcoming retreat.

(Continued on next page)

Bamboo palm
Lady palm
Chinese fountain palm

When palms came indoors *in the late 1800's, no Victorian parlor was complete without one. Still unsurpassed for bold silhouette, they make splendid choices for both single and group plant settings. Here is a guide to the eight palms you'll most likely find at nurseries and plant shops. From left to right they are* Archontophoenix cunninghamiana *(Seaforthia elegans, king palm held by Victorian woman),* Phoenix roebelenii *(pigmy date palm),* Howea forsterana *(paradise palm),* Caryota urens *(fishtail wine palm),* Chamaedorea elegans *(Neanthe bella, parlor palm),* Chamaedorea seifrizii *(bamboo palm),* Livistona chinensis *(Chinese fountain palm), and* Rhapis excelsa *(lady palm).*

...At Home with Plants

Display: Making the most of plants & places

In the great houses of the Victorian era, there were conservatories, greenhouses, and orangeries—elegant pavilions where exotic trees and ferns lived in splendor, protected from inclement weather. Each plant was given its own space, its own pedestal, to show off its handsomeness. Rare and flowering botanicals were brought in from private greenhouses at the peak of their magnificence to be given star treatment.

We grow stately palms and delicate orchids simply by sharing our living spaces with their drama, their sculptural forms. But *how* we share is a leaf to be borrowed from the Victorians' book. A fern is a fern until it is given center stage: place a single full Boston fern atop a polished mahogany pedestal, and instantly it is a personality. A collection of silver Revere bowls, each with a sassy pot of dwarf marigolds brought indoors for a special occasion, to parade up the edge of a wood staircase . . . a Japanese wooden hibachi holding a lush, glossy ivy . . . a tall-stalked amaryllis, its beauty reflected in an oval oak-framed mirror . . these are today's star treatments for performing plants. You'll see a galaxy of ideas on pages 12–63.

A single plant can be a display on its own, or it can crown a display of nonplant objects. But whatever you do, if the plant is beautiful, give it the importance it deserves.

Do you have a window seat? Put it to work as a stage for plants. Lifting plants off the floor gives them emphasis, and collecting them in one area gives them community transpiration —plants that live together grow better together.

Color & pattern

Plant foliage is incredibly diverse in pattern and color, encompassing countless variations in tone and shade, from chartreuse to deep forest green.

So your choice of plant color can be an important one in coordinating greenery with your personal decorating scheme.

Against pale walls or wallpaper, a light-colored plant might fade into the background. Similarly, dark-leafed plants do not find compatible display against very dark walls. The more subtle the plant color, the more suited it is for setting against a highly decorative background.

Some leaves have particularly intricate patterns; they appear variegated, mottled, prominently veined, or outlined with one or more contrasting colors. Such plants may make a room look cluttered if you use too many of them, but a few can lend interest and life to a grouping of greenery. Areas where this is truly effective are the built-in planter, garden room, and room divider. Individually, heavily patterned leaf plants are good subjects for accenting such confined spaces as a small bedside table or alcove.

Buyer's guide to healthy plants

When you have an urge to buy a house plant, you need to consider two things: the plant itself and the shop or nursery where it's sold. Be choosy; don't settle for the first plant you see.

Finding a reputable house plant dealer is the first step. You may have good luck with bargain plants, especially if you buy from a department where there is rapid turnover of plants. But if you need advice and information, it may be best to buy from a nursery, plant boutique, or florist shop. In any case, buy where you feel certain the plants are given proper treatment.

Survey the general plant selection. Do most of the plants seem healthy and happy? Overall excellence of products usually signifies good merchandise and proper care of house plants.

Look at the plant itself. Does it look healthy? Is it free from leaf damage and pests? Is the color good? Does it have a pleasing shape? Is the leaf size consistent? Does it show any new growth? If the answer to all these questions is "Yes," your choice is probably a good one.

Check to see if the plant is potbound. If any plant roots are peeking through the drainage hole, the plant may have been in that pot for too long. It's best to choose a different plant or plan to repot it at home immediately.

Choose a plant the size you want it. If you want a large house plant, don't buy a small version and wait for it to grow—it could take months or years. A larger plant that is better established will not only give the effect you want, but should also adapt to a new environment more readily.

Pretty as a picture
A fine Paphiopedilum (lady's slipper) re-peats not only the colors but the mood of this painting. Such simple settings are often the most striking and memorable. Design: Tosca Schalberg.

Two beauties
Matching lacquered baskets hold pots of Spathiphyllum 'Clevelandii', a favorite plant for its ability to grow in poor light month after month. If given good light, this plant will stay in nearly constant bloom.

Bedside cheer
Cissus antarctica *(kangaroo treebine), ensconced in brass bowl containers, top wrought-iron stands. The glossy green foliage complements the leaf designs in rich wall fabrics and bedspread. Design: Martha Baum and Sharon Marston.*

Decorating with Plants

Plants are far more than mere ornaments on the home decorating scene. They can play a functional, everyday role in home interior decorating, and when this happens, both plant and home are enhanced. This colorful section of *Decorating with Indoor Plants* is devoted to introducing a myriad of ideas on how you can best incorporate plants into your personal way of life, ideas from the ultracontemporary to the more traditional. Ninety-four color photographs display plants as individuals—proud specimen plants whose very presence in a room earns comment—and plants in groups, making garden rooms brim with healthy plant life that brings the great outdoors inside.

In this section we demonstrate the use of blossoming seasonal plants for attention-getting centerpieces, as well as more permanent displays of plants that highlight tables and chests. Plants—nature's art forms—are pictured along with paintings, antiques, and sculpture, actually matching moods and repeating shapes and colors as living extensions of the manmade art. Plants and fireplaces, plants and windows, plants in kitchens and bathrooms and hallways, plants on stairways . . . we've explored open spaces, nooks and crannies, even dark places requiring artificial lighting, and discovered to our delight that plants are showing up as important decorations in every conceivable area of today's homes.

Accompanying the decorating ideas are useful tips on how to hang plants, on the types and uses of various containers, and on growing plants in the tiniest greenhouse yet, the window greenhouse.

Appreciating a plant's decorative value and what it can do for a room is what this section is all about. We hope it will serve as inspiration for your decorating goals.

A meeting of plants
Dressed up for home entertaining is a window-filling Ficus benjamina. *Luxuriant white chrysanthemums decorate the tree's slender trunk, their pots concealed within a woven wool sleeve. Design: Robert Browning.*

Tea time
How to turn a delicious little scene into something extraordinary? To a table set for tea time, add splendid Saintpaulia ionantha *(African violets), double potted in a silver Revere bowl whose glossy underside is reflected in a mirror.*

Candlelight and cyclamen
At first glimpse this turn-of-the-century Chinese brass container would not seem deep enough for plantings, but the shallow-rooted cyclamen suits it well. These beauties were transplanted from their growing pots into the container, which is protected from moisture by a double lining of foil.

Herbal treat
Allium tuberosum *(garlic chives) are planted directly into a plastic-lined* pâté en croûte *pan with light tuckings of sphagnum moss to conceal the soil. Finishing touches are* escargot *shells—sans snails.*

A still life to remember
Artfully crafted ceramic wears well in the botanical world. Here a Ficus deltoidea *(mistletoe fig) is housed in a highly glazed container with matching saucer.*

Containers

When you use indoor plants as an integral part of your decor—either as major points of interest or as accents—the successful matchup of plant and pot becomes an important consideration. There's no denying that containers are decorative elements. And since they also provide the environment for plants to grow in, it is wise to select your pots carefully, with some solid background information in mind.

Containers should form a balanced base for plants, both visually and actually. A too-small pot gives a plant a top-heavy look and cramped growing quarters. A too-large pot overpowers the plant, making it seem undernourished and unloved; it can also lead to a plant's demise.

Here are some simple guidelines for matching containers to plants:

• For branching or shrubby plants, the width of the foliage should be two to three times the width of the pot.

• For low-growing, spreading plants, the foliage can be from two to six times the pot's width.

• For trees and other tall plants, use your eye. The container should create a base that looks substantial and is substantial—one the cat can't knock over.

• Whether you plant directly in the decorative container or use it as a decorative sleeve (see page 17), the new pot should be no more than 2 inches wider than the nursery container.

Containers as room accessories

When you're looking for plant containers, keep in mind the color scheme of your room, the style of the furniture, and the look of the plant itself. If you plan to group several plants, try to find matching or compatible containers to help unify the collection.

Should you feel uncertain about which kind of container to use in a room, remember that simple shapes and neutral colors will work in most situations.

What's available in containers?

Thanks to today's emphasis on indoor plants, a wide variety of containers can be found at nurseries, indoor plant shops, garden supply stores, antique shops, craft shops, hardware and home accessories stores, fairs, or anywhere else that garden or house plant supplies are sold.

Whenever possible, purchase the plant and its container—with a matching or suitable drip saucer, if needed (see page 18)—at the same time. With the plant in hand, it's much simpler to judge the container's and saucer's size, style, and compatibility.

Choose a container with your plant's growing habits in mind. A fast-growing indoor plant will need a larger pot than a slow grower.

Following is a discussion of the different types of containers, some more readily available than others.

Clay pots. A long-standing favorite of gardeners, the clay pot is inexpensive and available in a great range of shapes and sizes. The earthy color blends nicely with many furniture styles and gives an understated background to plants.

Because they are porous, clay pots absorb moisture and permit air circulation, making it difficult (but not impossible) to overwater plants growing in them.

If plants are overfertilized, excess salts can form a telltale white crust on the container sides. And in areas where the water has a heavy salt concentration, the excess salts leach out, also forming a white crust on pot sides. A nonporous container cannot give you these distress signals. Because clay pots can, they're especially useful for beginning gardeners.

Plastic pots. Containers made of plastic, either rigid or rubbery, are easy to clean, lightweight even when watered, inexpensive, and sold in a variety of colors, shapes, and sizes. Some are made of clear plastic, exposing the potting mix and root systems.

Nonporous plastic pots may create a watering problem: they neither absorb moisture nor permit air circulation, so overwatering and rotting roots are dangers.

On the other hand, since watered plants in plastic pots remain moist longer than plants in porous containers and need watering less frequently, plastic pots are the best choice for moisture-loving plants.

Glazed ceramic pots. Purchasable in many colors or vividly

Plant containers *come in an exciting variety of shapes, styles, and materials, from the strictly utilitarian to the highly decorative and even whimsical. Select containers that enhance both the appearance of your room and the plants that they hold.*

decorated, glazed ceramic pots are quite ornamental. Prices vary according to size and decoration; ceramic pots that are imported will often carry higher price tags; so will those that are antiques.

Glazed containers, like plastic pots, are nonporous and may present watering problems to the novice. If you find the perfect glazed pot but are hesitant to buy it because of possible watering difficulties, use it as a decorative sleeve (see page 17).

Metal containers. Plants displayed in containers of copper, brass, silver, pewter, polished steel, iron, or aluminum can add just the right touch of elegance or country sophistication.

For various reasons, most metal containers are best used as decorative sleeves. Since many metals tarnish, these containers may require periodic cleaning or polishing, which is more easily done if the plant is lifted out. And if excess water is left standing indefinitely in the pot, it

could corrode the metals, so you'll want to line a valuable container with heavy plastic or place a drainage saucer inside to avoid water damage.

Metal containers rarely have drainage holes. If you decide to plant directly into your metal pot, add a layer of drainage material (see page 70) to capture any excess moisture created by regular waterings. If you're lucky enough to find a metal pot with proper drainage holes, treat it as a normal container when planting. Be sure to provide a compatible saucer to catch any water runoff.

Plant roots that touch the sides or bottom of a copper pot will die. This shouldn't radically affect the plant's health, since the remaining roots will live.

Baskets. Plants and baskets make fine companions. Baskets can be found in a profusion of shapes, sizes, and price ranges. Though usually woven of natural materials in shades of beige or brown, some are painted or stained in a delightful variety of colors.

Since baskets aren't watertight,

they should be used as decorative sleeves. Unless a saucer can be placed inside the basket, watered plants will leak, possibly ruining furniture surfaces and eventually the basket.

A few baskets can be purchased with metal or plastic inserts, permitting planting in them directly. Since these inserts do not have drainage holes, you should treat them as drainless containers when planting.

Wooden containers. Though more commonly used outdoors, wooden containers can come indoors too. They are relatively inexpensive and available in lots of sizes, shapes, and wood types.

Stained, varnished, or painted wood is usually nonporous; untreated wood containers can be porous. If drainage holes are present, place a waterproof saucer under the pot to catch excess water.

...Containers

If your wooden container is slatted, the sides may not be waterproof. This could create a seepage problem that would be unattractive, as well as being hard on furniture surfaces. It's best to use wooden containers as decorative sleeves rather than planting in them directly.

Eclectic containers. Many interesting, creative plantings result from using containers originally designed for other uses. A teacup, soup tureen, cooky jar, pitcher, coffee pot, watering can, or anything else with enough space to hold potting mix and a plant can be transformed into a unique container. You need only imagination and boldness to carry it off.

Either use these containers as decorative sleeves or follow the directions for planting in drainless containers (see page 70).

Decorative sleeves

A decorative sleeve is any container that an already-potted house plant is set into for display purposes. The decorative sleeve has many advantages:

• Valuable or easily damaged containers are protected from bad effects of direct planting.

• A sick plant can be replaced quickly by a healthy one.

• Many decorative sleeves are watertight, eliminating the need for a drip saucer or tray.

• If you display plants in a poor growing location, such as a dark hall, you can rotate several plants between a good growing location and a decorative sleeve placed in a spot with insufficient light.

Using decorative sleeves is easy. The sleeve should be at least an inch larger in diameter than the plant's container to allow for good air circulation. Put the potted indoor plant into the sleeve. If the plant sits too low,

Decorative sleeves *display potted plants. From left: layer of pebbles supports potted plant inside sleeve; brick raises plant just short of sleeve rim; stacked clay pots lift plant to top of wicker basket.*

... *Containers*

prop it up with bricks, other clay pots turned upside down, layers of small rocks or pebbles, sphagnum moss, empty aluminum food cans, wooden blocks, or any other material that will raise the plant to proper level.

If the runoff from normal watering could damage your decorative sleeve, line it with heavy plastic or provide a drip saucer inside the sleeve under the potted plant.

Some indoor gardeners also line the space between the pot and the sleeve to give the illusion of direct planting. Sphagnum moss or pebbles are commonly used; loosely packed, they still permit adequate air circulation around the container. A top dressing of pebbles, bark, or sphagnum moss covering the soil surface of both the plant and the liner helps add to this illusion (see "Finishing touches," on this page).

Catch that drip!

Even if you correctly water a house plant growing in a container that has proper drainage, you're going to have drips. Any excess water the potting mix can't retain during normal watering will run out the drainage holes. Wherever you display house plants, this runoff may be troublesome. The most efficient solution is to provide a saucer to catch the excess water.

Whenever possible, buy a drip saucer or tray at the same time you purchase a container. Many containers are sold with matching saucers. If not, it's up to the indoor gardener to find something suitable. Look for unobtrusive or compatible saucers or trays. Though any saucer can protect furniture surfaces, one that is hopelessly mismatched can ruin the visual effect of the house plant.

Part of the runoff problem can be solved at watering time. Take house plants to a sink for watering; then let them drain in the sink for at least 10 minutes. This will take care of the majority of excess water, but it doesn't eliminate the need for a drip saucer.

If your drip saucer or tray is made of a porous material, such as clay, it too can absorb moisture. You can waterproof the drip saucer with a silicone paint, eliminating the absorption problem. Water sitting even in nonporous saucers, such as plastic or glazed ceramic, may cause condensation on the outside, and if the saucer remains in one spot long enough, the contact may eventually ruin furniture surfaces or rot carpets.

Many indoor gardeners protect surfaces by putting "spacers" between drip saucers and furniture, floors, or carpets. Spacers create a buffer zone, an air space in which any absorbed moisture or moisture caused by condensation can be dissipated. Coasters, mats, blocks of wood, metal or wooden plant holders, or any

other means of raising the plant container and saucer off furniture or carpet can serve this purpose, helping to eliminate the chance of water damage.

Finishing touches

Trees and other upright-growing floor plants leave the potting soil exposed to view. If you find the exposed soil unattractive, you can use a top dressing or plant a ground cover as camouflage.

Pebbles, marble chips, decorative bark, and sphagnum moss are good choices for top dressing. A thin layer of any of these will not only hide the soil surface but will also help the soil retain moisture.

You will need to soak sphagnum moss to make it manageable. Place the moss in boiling water, let it cool for several hours, squeeze out excess water, then spread a thin layer over the soil surface. Be sure to keep the moss layer moist once it's in place; if sphagnum moss dries out, it may be hard to remoisten.

A living ground cover is a neat touch for trees or other large plants that have enough exposed soil surface. *Ficus pumila* (creeping fig) and *Soleirolia soleirolii* (baby's tears) make a good living mulch. Just be sure the ground cover and the tree or large plant have compatible needs for light, temperature, and water. The Plant Selection Guide starting on page 74 will help.

Desk-top miniature
Three minute clay pots holding Hedera helix (English ivy) make nice nesters for an antique brass box.

Animal sculptures make whimsical plant containers as well as conversation pieces. This show-stopping unicorn contains Adiantum tenerum (maidenhair fern), double potted for plant rotation and special care. Horticultural design: Plantco.

Harmonious setting
A potted Hedera helix (English ivy) and its saucer join company with a small-legged, handwoven basket from the Philippines.

Plant Stands

Put your plant on a pedestal—fancy old-fashioned wicker, antique Italian wrought iron, or a modern, mirrored cube—and you give it importance, visibility, a chance to be truly graceful. Plants on stands are likely to enjoy good health. They have room to grow in every direction and are easy to move about for sunning and watering. But watering can ruin some stand tops. Either use a waterproof drip saucer or take the plant to the sink, letting it drain completely before replacing it. Pretty plant choices for stands are those that spread or dangle, such as ferns, ivies, and spider plants.

Plant pillar
A simple and solid block of wood, painted white to blend with the walls, gives the impression of a plant suspended in space. The tendrils of an Epipremnum aureum *(devil's ivy, silver pothos) dangle down the sides of the stand, creating a unifying feeling between it and a* Dieffenbachia maculata *(dumb cane). Horticultural design: Plantco.*

Spider kingdom
Prolific plants, such as this grand old Chlorophytum comosum *(spider plant), often require special accommodations. A perfect alternative to hanging the plant is this glass and brass stand, measuring in at 5 feet tall.*

Handsome twosome
A wooden plant stand fashioned after a bar stool does the work of two plant perches. On the lower level is a bright and bushy Tripogandra multiflora *(bridal veil); above it, a young* Ficus benjamina *sits in a wallpaper-complementing ceramic pot.*

Upstairs, downstairs
An antique ladder is both utilitarian and eye pleasing when its steps are used for displaying plants. Top to bottom are a Tripogandra multiflora *(bridal veil),* Tillandsia *(a bromeliad),* Aeschynanthus radicans *(lipstick plant), and* Tillandsia. *Design: Beth Dunbar.*

Elephant ride
Asplenium bulbiferum (mother fern) is displayed to best advantage riding a plump ceramic elephant. Plant and stand tie in beautifully with the colors and design of the Oriental carpet.

Healthy hanger
An exuberant Cissus antarctica *(kangaroo treebine) is suspended in a wide-rimmed Japanese rice basket that gives balance and support to the broad, trailing plant. Below is a* Dracaena deremensis.

Petite wall hanger
A plastic-lined basket gets filled with spagnum moss over which a sheet of chicken wire is attached. Several tiny Polygonum capitatum *(knotweed) plants are gently tucked through the wire, with bits of the moss to dress the roots. The result: A temporary display for a guest bedroom or bath, certain to retain its beauty indoors for a week or so.*

Kitchen drama
An island of greenery is created by a magnificent Nephrolepis exaltata 'Bostoniensis' *(Boston fern) hanging from a vintage meat hanger over a retired antique chopping block. A skylight fulfills all the plant's needs for light. Design: Sherri Waldman.*

Hanging Plants

Immediately striking you with their graceful foliage and dramatic form, plants suspended in the air take on a special perspective: they are showpieces in the round. To many plant lovers, especially those with small living quarters, the air provides a fine home for plants, freeing valuable floor or counter space. In addition to saving space, hanging plants offer a convenient solution to decorating problems, softening harsh wall surfaces, defining living areas, and filling empty corners. Whether you begin with one or several, hanging plants will give you a delightful swinging garden overhead.

Any indoor plant with a dangling or spreading habit can be hung to advantage. Possible locations are in or around windows, filling spaces on empty walls or in corners, and around skylights. Just be sure to hang the plants out of the way of foot traffic—bumping into a heavy hanging plant isn't healthy for the person or the plant!

You'll face two major challenges with hanging plants: how to suspend the plant and how to water it once it's up. Whenever possible, use plastic pots for your hanging plants; they weigh much less than clay or ceramic pots and absorb no moisture so plants in them require less water. Most plants suitable for hanging will cover the container with foliage, so you needn't worry about spoiling your decor. If your plant does need a decorative container, be sure to choose one that's waterproof.

Hanging how-tos

If your ceiling has exposed beams or is paneled with wood that is at least ¾ inch thick, you can probably just screw a hook into it wherever you want to suspend a plant. Many ceilings and walls, however, are made of gypsum board or plaster over lath, and these alone will not hold the threads of a screw securely enough to prevent it from pulling loose when a plant is attached. You're much better off locating a ceiling joist or a wall stud (usually 2 by 4s, 2 by 6s, or 2 by 8s) beneath the plaster or gypsum board for a support. Once you locate the joist or stud, carefully drill a pilot hole, then screw in a hook that's long enough to penetrate both the ceiling or wall material and the joist or stud.

To find a ceiling joist or wall stud, measure 14½ inches out from a major corner; succeeding joists or studs should fall every 16 inches (though in some buildings, joists and studs are 20 or 24 inches apart). Keep in mind that joists run in one direction only, so measure from the corner along both walls to be sure to locate one. If you don't locate a joist or stud at this location, try the corners at the opposite end of the wall, and then work back.

Other methods of locating covered framework are to use a stud finder (a magnetic device available in hardware stores; it actually finds nails, not studs) or to knock firmly on the ceiling or wall with the heel of your fist. A solid sound means you've located a joist or stud; a hollow sound tells you to keep looking. Whichever method you use, drill a small hole or tap in a small nail to be sure you've actually located a joist or stud.

(Continued on next page)

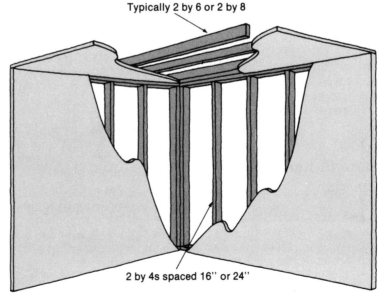

Typically 2 by 6 or 2 by 8

2 by 4s spaced 16" or 24"

Ceiling joists and wall studs *offer best support for hanging plants. Joists and studs are located behind plaster or gypsum board; find them by measuring or tapping on wall or ceiling.*

... *Hanging Plants*

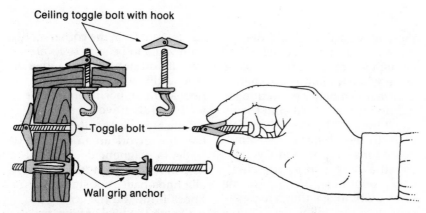

Ceiling toggle bolt with hook

—Toggle bolt—

Wall grip anchor

These fasteners *require a predrilled hole in wall or ceiling. Use them to support medium to lightweight containers—not more than 9 inches in diameter.*

If you want to place a plant hanger on a spot on the wall that doesn't have a stud, try using a plastic or lead "sleeve" available at hardware stores. Placed in a predrilled hole, the sleeve expands to create a binding fit when you insert a screw into it. Sleeves don't work in ceilings, but toggle bolts, also available at hardware stores, will do the job there as well as on the wall. Sleeve fasteners and toggle bolts are illustrated above.

Where to hang your plant

Windows are favored locations for hanging plants because they provide good light. (There are artificial lighting units for hanging plants, but many people find them unattractive.) If you want the good light provided by a sunny window but know your plant can't tolerate it, suspend the plant to the side of the window. For convenience, hang plants far enough away from windows to allow opening and closing of windows, curtains, or draperies.

Locations away from windows may or may not provide enough light for hanging plants. Generally speaking, a location that has enough indirect light for you to read comfortably for an hour or two without turning on a lamp should also provide enough light for most indoor plants.

Keep an eye out for signs of spindly growth or dropping leaves on hanging plants; these signs can mean your plant is receiving inadequate light. In dark corners or other locations that receive low levels of light, try plants that can adapt to these situations. Plants that will survive in low light are listed in the charts on pages 74–79.

Water & the hanging plant

Watering a hanging plant can be a challenge. A watered plant will drip, presenting a threat to floors, rugs, and furniture. You can prevent drips by providing a drip saucer to catch the water (some plastic hanging containers have attached saucers; or buy a tray that clips onto the bottom of hanging pots). Other solutions are to use a waterproof container as a decorative sleeve (see page 17), or to take the hanging plant down to water it and let it drain completely before rehanging it.

Plants that like to hang

Following is a list of plants that grow attractively in hanging containers. We have listed both the botanical name and—in parentheses—the common name for each plant.

By no means should you feel limited to suspending just the plants listed here. Since nurseries are constantly trying new ideas (and since plant availability varies in different parts of the country), you may well find exciting new ideas on your own.

Excellent choice *for hanging plant is* Aeschynanthus radicans *(lipstick plant). Like lipsticks from their cases, tubular red 2-inch flowers emerge from purplish black flower tubes.*

Abutilon megapotamicum (flowering maple, Chinese bellflower)

Aeschynanthus radicans (lipstick plant)

Alloplectus nummularia (goldfish plant)

Asparagus densiflorus 'Sprengeri' (Sprenger asparagus)

Ceropegia woodii (rosary vine)

Chlorophytum comosum (spider plant)

Cissus antarctica (kangaroo treebine)

Cissus rhombifolia (grape ivy)

Clerodendrum thomsoniae (bleeding heart glorybower)

Coleus hybridus (coleus)

Columnea 'Stavanger' (Norse fire plant)

Davallia trichomanoides (squirrel's foot fern)

Epiphyllum (orchid cactus)

Epipremnum aureum (devil's ivy, silver pothos)

Episcia cupreata (flame violet)

Ficus pumila (creeping fig)

Fittonia verschaffeltii (fittonia)

Gynura aurantiaca (purple velvet plant)

Hedera species (ivies)

Hoya bella (miniature wax plant)

Hoya carnosa (wax plant)

Humata tyermannii (bear's foot fern)

Lysimachia nummularia (creeping Jennie)

Maranta leuconeura (prayer plant, rabbit tracks)

Nephrolepis exaltata (sword fern)

Nephrolepis exaltata 'Bostoniensis' (Boston fern)

Nicodemia diversifolia (indoor oak)

Ornithogalum caudatum (pregnant onion)

Philodendron scandens oxycardium (heart-leaf philodendron)

Platycerium bifurcatum (staghorn fern)

Plectranthus australis (creeping Charlie, Swedish ivy)

Rhipsalidopsis gaertneri (Easter cactus)

Saxifraga stolonifera (strawberry geranium)

Schlumbergera bridgesii (Christmas cactus)

Sedum morganianum (donkey tail)

Senecio rowleyanus (string of beads)

Stephanotis floribunda (Madagascar jasmine)

Syngonium podophyllum (arrowhead vine)

Tolmiea menziesii (piggy-back plant)

Tradescantia fluminensis (wandering Jew)

Tripogandra multiflora (bridal veil)

Zebrina pendula (wandering Jew)

Built-in Planters

For many lovers of indoor plants, abundance is an assurance of bliss. Falling short of creating a virtual jungle, built-in planters give enthusiasts a means of collecting numerous plants for one special corner of the home. And by consolidating them, owners can avoid the sprawl—one plant here, one plant there—that makes plant maintenance a chore.

Many built-in planters can sustain large plants and trees that command attention by their sheer size, bringing gardening indoors on a truly dramatic scale. Smaller, off-the-floor planters can decorate balconies, stairways, windows, and other areas of the home.

Creating a lush interior garden can be a rewarding and uncomplicated experience. Whether your planter was developed as an integral part of your home's architecture or you decided to install one later, the basic requirements are the same: ample natural light, well-draining soil, adequate soil depth, and some disciplined gardening—notably pruning to keep plants under control, and replacing any plants that grow too large for the house.

Light—the determining factor

A really successful built-in planter depends on ample amounts of natural light. The most efficient way to supply light is to position the planter directly under or adjacent to a skylight.

A large skylight gives the best light since it encourages plants to grow upward instead of leaning sideways toward a light source. Another method of providing light is to place the planter as close as possible to large windows, glass doors, or a window wall. Without sufficient light, large plants especially would fade, then slowly die.

You can use artificial lighting to supplement the natural light, but artificial light alone will probably be inadequate to sustain a large planting. Built-in planters are also candidates for dramatic lighting; for more information, see pages 32–33.

Soil & soil depth

Whether your built-in planter opens to the ground below the house or is built on top of the floor, you'll want an adequate soil depth, a loose soil mix, and drainage material. For most large plants, you'll need a soil depth of at least 2 feet, as well as several inches of drainage material.

Premixed sacked potting soil is available in nurseries or garden centers. The mix is easy to handle and works well in large planters. Use a commercial mix specifically formulated for house plants. It temporarily provides the nutrients that plants need; you can replenish these nutrients when necessary with a house plant fertilizer. The packaged potting mix has been sterilized to eliminate any pests or diseases. You can also make your own soil mix; directions are on page 67.

Gravel makes a good drainage material; it too is available from nurseries or garden centers. A topping of mulch, such as ground bark, will help the soil retain moisture.

If your planter sits directly on the floor or subfloor, be sure the planter is watertight.

Indoor landscaping

Most built-in planter gardens rely on large plants with striking foliage to create the focal point, with low-growing foliage plants tucked in to camouflage the soil.

Large plants from the ficus family—such as *Ficus benjamina*, *Ficus elastica* (rubber plant), or *Ficus lyrata* (fiddleleaf fig)—or any of the larger palm trees are frequently chosen for planter focus because of their interesting shape or elegant foliage.

All plants sharing the environment of a planter garden should have similar growing requirements. When you select ground cover plants, keep in mind that they'll grow in the shadow of larger plants, so look for low-growing foliage plants that prefer low light.

What about flower color?

While permanent plantings in most built-in planters depend on indoor trees and large foliage plants, you can add seasonal spots of color. Pots of flowering plants can be sunk up to their container rims in the soil mix to perk up your green garden. When the flowers are spent, just remove the containers.

Tiled garden

Light-shedding skylights are mirrored in a window behind a perfect Ficus benjamina *in this high-ceilinged plant and music room. The planter opens to the ground below the house, providing soil depth for root systems. The glazed tiles make watering easy and safe. Design: George Cody. Horticultural design: Bill Derringer.*

Heidi revisited

An indoor window box is a bright addition to a rustic bedroom loft. Furry tendrils of Asparagus densiflorus 'Sprengeri' *(Sprenger asparagus) spill over the wooden container's sides to be viewed from the living room below. Skylights provide illumination for growth. Design: Louise S. Stewart.*

Green on white

Linking a bright white living room with a stairway leading to a lower level, a built-in planter contains an exuberant splash of green with pots of Spathiphyllum 'Clevelandii' *and* Cissus rhombifolia *(grape ivy).*

Garden Rooms

Plant rooms give you a garden atmosphere indoors, all through the year. Though some plant rooms are specially designed for the well-being of plants—rooms with skylights, glass walls or roofs, built-in watering and drainage systems—still others are converted porches, breezeways, and attics. The main requirement for a successful garden room is good light that can accommodate a large group of plants. Furnish your garden room with natural accompaniments for plant life: rattan, wicker, or rustproofed wrought iron that will be resistant to humidity and water stains. Keep precious wood surfaces well away from watering regimens.

Inside, outside
A window wall blends a wealth of interior foliage with the forest outside. On opposite ends of the Oriental rug are a giant Ficus benjamina *and a* Ficus rubiginosa *(rustyleaf fig). Design: Nancy Hewitt.*

Blissful botanics
Just French doors away from a sunny porch, a garden corner celebrates the green life with a Ficus benjamina, *a beautifully trained fuchsia (normally grown outdoors), and cymbidiums in matching straw baskets.*

Formal jungle
Resembling an old-fashioned conservatory, this garden room is perfectly equipped to pamper its jungle of hanging, vining, and floor plants. A glass roof and wall panels provide natural light; sink and brick flooring make watering and care more convenient. Design: Robert Chittock.

Wall tracery
A plant wall glorifies one end of a living room that was created when flagstone patio was roofed over. The coral-flowered vine is bougainvillea; the tall plants with white-streaked leaves are Dieffenbachia amoena *(dumb cane). Design: Edward Nelson.*

Window stage
Like so many performers, a line-up of plants acts in unison to create an exciting scene—in this case, a window garden. Backstage has a convenient pebble-filled panel that retains moisture, reducing the frequency of watering chores. From left to right the on-stage stars are a Ficus benjamina *(floor plant), two citrus plants,* Tolmiea menziesii *(piggy-back),* Agave americana *(century plant), fibrous begonia,* Euphorbia milii *(crown of thorns),* Pachypodium lamieri, Nephrolepis exaltata 'Bostoniensis' *(Boston fern),* Chamaedorea elegans *(Neanthe bella, parlor palm), another Boston fern, and* Dizygotheca elegantissima *(threadleaf false aralia); overhead are a* Hedera helix *(English ivy), yet another Boston fern, and a* Coleus hybridus *(coleus). Design: Philip L. Brown.*

Kitchen greenhouse
Platycerium bifurcatum *(staghorn fern) strikingly decorates the wall supporting a greenhouse window. Other plants are a great* Agave victoriae-reginae, *three scented-leaf geraniums, and sweet basil. Design: Cindy McNae.*

Garden of delights
A north-facing window celebrates the green world's splendid variety of color and form. On the top shelf, left to right, are Cissus rhombifolia *'Ellen Danika' (oak leaf ivy),* Pteris cretica *'Wimsettii', and a hydrangea. Second shelf holds, from left,* Caladium bicolor *(fancy-leafed caladium),* Maranta leuconeura *(prayer plant),* Davallia trichomanoides *(squirrel's foot fern), and* Polystichum polyblepharum *(Japanese lace fern). On the third shelf are cyclamen, three* Sinningia speciosa *(gloxinia),* Adiantum tenerum *(maidenhair fern), and* Paphiopedilum *(lady's slipper). Bottom shelf boasts two cinerarias,* Streptocarpus *(cape primrose), calceolaria, cyclamen, and three* Kalanchoe blossfeldiana. *Horticultural design: Plantco.*

Greenhouse Windows

Owning a greenhouse—even the smallest of them all, the greenhouse window—introduces exciting new dimensions to indoor gardening. These windows make a sunny atmosphere for nurturing indoor plants as well as those that are normally grown outside; under the right conditions they can inspire perennials to bloom all through the year. Build or attach your prefabricated greenhouse onto a prominent window frame so that the wonderful variety of plants it supports can be appreciated by all, inside and outside your home.

If space is a consideration, or if you'd like to try greenhouse gardening on a small scale before investing in a large walk-in structure, a window-size greenhouse may be for you.

Light-providing bay windows and dormers have always made acceptable miniature greenhouses. More recently, prefabricated greenhouses (also called "reach-in" greenhouses) that can be attached to outside window frames have come into popular use. Inexpensive, easy to install and maintain, these manufactured units fit over most standard window openings. To provide access to the greenhouse window, screens and original windows are removed.

You can install window greenhouses in as many windows as you wish. Whether it's one or ten, these wonderful additions to your home add substantially to the area for displaying and growing plants, and they do it without eating up space. A single four-shelved greenhouse window can hold as many as 25 small to medium-size potted plants.

Features & equipment

Generally constructed with rigid aluminum frames, prefabricated greenhouse windows have glass or heavy-gauge transparent plastic on the top and three outer sides, with the fourth side open to the room. Some manufacturers are using bronze-tinted solar glass roofs that screen ultraviolet light, which is plant-damaging in too-high doses.

A window greenhouse should come equipped with ventilators to admit fresh air to plant life. Some units have hinged top ventilators; others have sliding vents on the side panels. Make certain that all vents have insect screens, preferably removable ones.

These simple window sill stretchers require little additional equipment. In really frigid weather, you might want to use a small electric heater to keep your plants at a comfortable temperature. Otherwise, the heat from the house is usually sufficient to warm window greenhouses.

In an effort to better simulate a real greenhouse environment, at least one manufacturer has developed a built-in misting system with its own separate faucet. Humidity trays (purchasable at garden and hardware stores) are a practical and inexpensive investment for greenhouse windows, especially those with the most exposure to drying sun. When the trays are lined with pebbles, the pots resting in them need far less frequent watering.

Light considerations

One of the purposes of having a greenhouse window is to give your plants a bright place for growing. North-facing windows (unless heavily shaded by trees or buildings) provide good even light throughout the daylight hours, with no direct sun. Windows facing east or west offer intense light or direct sun in the morning or afternoon and less light during the rest of the day. Be sure to select plants that are suitable to these varying levels of sunlight.

South-facing windows generally receive the most sunlight for the greatest part of the day, giving you the opportunity to be successful with flowering plants and other sun lovers, such as cacti.

Whatever the exposure, keep foliage from actually touching the greenhouse walls; intense sun can burn foliage, and cold or freezing weather can injure tender plants. Pale or wilting foliage on a plant can indicate it's receiving too much light.

If you are uncertain as to which plants work best under different exposures, don't hesitate to consult the staff at your nursery or plant store.

Plants & Light

Nothing adds sparkle to a dim corner of the home like a living, growing plant. And yet, without adequate illumination, few plants can adapt to these locations. Many indoor gardeners rotate their plants between dark places and a good growing spot, while others simply replace light-deprived plants when they reach the point of no return. But the kindest method for maintaining plants in low-light or no-light situations is to provide them with artificial lighting. It will yield both growth and drama.

Indoor gardeners project artificial light onto their plants for two reasons: to provide supplemental or total light for plant growth and to highlight a specimen plant or a plant grouping. Whatever your purpose in plant lighting—be it for growth or strictly for drama—you'll find many light fixtures and systems available.

Artificial lights

If a location you choose for growing plants needs extra light, consider artificial illumination. Cool, white, power-thrifty fluorescent lights have long been used as sources of supplemental plant illumination. They can also be used in combination with incandescent light. Incandescent bulbs should not be used alone in dark areas, though; they are not strong enough in the red and blue color bands that plants require, and they generate too much heat for sensitive plants.

Some indoor gardeners grow plants totally under artificial lights. As long as that light provides the same intensity and quality of light found in natural sunlight, and your plants are exposed to it for a sufficient period each day, they should thrive.

Whether you buy a lighting unit or make one, provide some method of adjusting its height above the plant. Start with the tubes 6 to 12 inches above the foliage. If the stems bunch together unnaturally, the plants are

Incandescent bulbs *can't sustain a plant's total light needs, but can be used in combination with fluorescent lights or with frequent rotation of the plant to sunnier locations.*

receiving too much light. If leggy, they need more light.

Fixtures need a white or foil reflector to direct light onto plants. When placing plants under fluorescent light, remember that the light is strongest at the center of the tube. A standard amount of light for all plants is 15 to 20 watts of light for every square foot of growing surface.

Most foliage plants need 10 to 12 hours of light per day; flowering plants require 16. For all plants, a regular light exposure schedule is important to healthy growth. An inexpensive timer can regulate the lights.

New, slimmer fluorescent fixtures can be attached under cabinets or shelves to light plants in these dark spaces. You can also find tubes formulated for plant growth in this mini-size.

Downlights

Downlight is direct or directed lighting from above, shining down and creating pools of light surrounding a plant or plant grouping. Common downlight fixtures include recessed, semirecessed, and ceiling-mounted fixtures that appear to blend into the ceiling, as well as track light fixtures that can be aimed downward.

Once recessed or ceiling-mounted fixtures are installed, the illuminated area cannot be changed; be sure the place you've selected for a spotlighted tree is precisely where you want it.

To put your plant or plant grouping in the spotlight, fixtures can be placed just above the plant, spaced evenly over the spot to light a larger area, or aimed at the plant from a nearby track.

Uplights

Uplighting originates from canister or sphere fixtures placed below the highlighted plant or plant grouping, usually on the floor. Used effectively, uplights throw intriguing leafy shadow patterns on walls and ceilings.

Uplighting fixtures that generate a great deal of heat and are too near foliage or roots can damage your plants. Check with your hand—if it feels too hot for your hand, it's too close to the plant.

Perfect plant habitat

Two Ficus lyrata *(fiddleleaf figs) and* Neoregelia, *a bromeliad, bask in the gleam provided by a skylight. For special drama, day and night, ceiling beams are outfitted with lights aimed at both plants and the art that they enhance. Design: William Gaylord. Horticultural design: Baruch Himmilstein.*

Trees & Other Large Plants

Blank walls, empty corners, and high ceilings come alive when graced by trees and other large plants that bring the garden indoors.

Belying their high decorative impact, large plants are low-maintenance items. They require less fertilizer and lower light levels than many smaller house plants, since their major growth has usually occurred by the time they reach your home. Large plants need occasional dusting and grooming; they must have regular watering, and you'll need to use waterproof saucers to protect floors and rugs—ordinary clay saucers won't do. Otherwise, you can treat your trees and large plants like pieces of art or furniture.

Trees as room dividers
A forest of Ficus benjamina *in different sizes defines the boundaries between living room and dining room, yet allows for a sense of airiness, openness. Design: Gayle Holmes.*

Impact tree
This grand old Yucca gloriosa *(Spanish dagger) is appreciated for its stately form—stark lines of a straight trunk culminating in a burst of deep green leaves. It is best described as sculpturesque, best placed in a spacious, sunlit room. Design: Michael Taylor.*

Ficus and friends
Trees with spindly trunks and sparse low foliage such as this Ficus benjamina *are well suited to groupings with smaller plants. Here* Cissus rhombifolia *(grape ivy) surrounds the large pot with leaves of a similar shade and shape. Design: Gayle Holmes.*

Green canopy
Ficus carica *(edible fig) and* Ficus lyrata *(fiddleleaf fig) bring nature indoors. Climbing to the ceiling, they create a cool, green canopy over a cozy living room setting. Design: Robert Bell.*

...Trees & Other Large Plants

Perky filler
With its fullness and spunkiness, Schefflera actinophylla (Queensland umbrella, octopus tree) makes a perfect corner tree. Windows on opposite walls give this one good light, ventilation.

Green fellowship
Ficus lyrata (*fiddleleaf fig*) is a highly effective indoor plant for a contemporary house with ultrahigh ceilings. Its coffee table companion is Beaucarnea recurvata (*ponytail, bottle palm*). Design: William Gaylord. Horticultural design: Baruch Himmelstein.

Seeing double
Totally in harmony with the symmetrical character of this living room are look-alike Arecastrum romanzoffianum *(queen palms) potted in matching baskets and positioned in line with sofas. A* Schefflera actinophylla *(Queensland umbrella, octopus tree) resides behind the sofa to the right and faces a small* Ficus benjamina. *On the chest is an* Epipremnum aureum *(pothos). Design: Kenneth R. Fehrman Interior Design, Inc.*

Trees as furniture
An exquisite specimen tree such as this Polyscias fruticosa 'Elegans' *(Ming aralia) confidently graces a corner like a rare, beloved chest or table. Design: Dorothy Knecht.*

Halls, Entries, Stairways

Plants make cheery companions for the "traveling" areas of your home—halls, stairways, and foyers. Select plants of the right size, shape, and character to adorn these spaces—a tall, slender *Ficus benjamina,* for example, fares well in a narrow hallway; a cactus or other sticky, grabby plants might be liabilities. Because these are frequently low-light areas, you'll need to choose plants that can adapt, or rotate sun lovers between here and brighter locations. And make certain that no plant becomes an obstacle people can trip over, especially on stairs.

Surprise landing
The luscious pinks and greens of a cymbidium give life and color to a quietly neutral stair landing. Flowering best in good light, the plant gets frequent trips to a sunny location. Design: Dorothy Knecht.

High society
Elegant French dolls sit musing in a hallway-turned-fashionable-parlor, complete with Oriental rug and luxuriant foliage of Chlorophytum comosum (spider plant) and Asplenium bulbiferum (mother fern). Design: Fred and Bobbie Kleinman.

The grandest entry
An enormous and delightful greeting for guests comes from a Livistona chinensis *(Chinese fountain palm), its great fans swaying some 3 feet beyond the chest and into the wide hallway. The skylight provides all light requirements. Design: Michael Taylor.*

Happiness in numbers
Basket after basket of potted Spathiphyllum *'Clevelandii' breaks the monotony of a long, monochromatic hallway and acts as a low-level screen to glass-paneled doors. Horticultural design: Plantco.*

Flowered stairway
A visual delight, tuberous begonias and impatiens in lively blue and white pots offer a floral mix and complement the tiles of a Mexico-influenced stairway.

In total harmony
A beautifully formed Ficus benjamina *gently towers over wicker chairs and game table, complementing the earth tones of the setting. Design: Michael Taylor.*

Visions of a florist shop
Scores of pink and white geraniums flower the year around in this exquisite hall gallery. A fruit-laden citrus plant and a pink Sinningia speciosa *(gloxinia) add still more color, complementing the cool dark green of a large* Hedera helix *(English ivy) floor plant.*

Kitchens

The busy kitchen, center of domestic life, can provide a nurturing environment for growing plants. Light, humidity, and good ventilation are generally in abundant supply, and the proximity of the sink encourages good watering habits. Here's the place to give your plants a washing—they like a sudsy bath and pests don't; use a small amount of mild soap and cool water. Keep your green friends well away from cooktops and ovens, where heat and fumes could do them damage. Great kitchen standbys are these humidity lovers: spider plants, ivies, wandering Jews, ferns, and herbs.

Esthetic organizer
Plants wear well almost everywhere, even in a reproduction of an antique berry box. In tiny pots are sedum, Asparagus setaceus *(fern asparagus), and the petite white annual* sweet alyssum. *Design: Rela Gleason.*

Greenhouse kitchen
This kitchen supports healthy plant life, with its angled windows along one wall, skylights overhead, and a pulley system that brings the plants down for watering. The happy hangers are Nephrolepis exaltata 'Bostoniensis' *(Boston fern),* Tradescantia albiflora *(wandering Jew), and* Chlorophytum comosum *(spider plant). On the counter is a* Tolmiea menziesii *(piggy-back). Design: Obie Bowman.*

...Kitchens

The low-light counter
A Hoya carnosa *(wax flower, wax plant) manages quite well on this counter with very little light.* Hoya *will not blossom under such conditions, but it can be appreciated for its glossy green foliage alone. A number of other plants can also thrive in low-light conditions—see the Plant Selection Guide, starting on page 74, for suggestions.*

Pot of another kind
Imagination is all it takes to come up with unique plant containers. Appropriate for kitchen display is a Selaginella kraussiana *(moss fern, spike moss) planted in a white ceramic soufflé dish.*

Reigning giant
A kitchen with great height and counter space can accommodate a giant or two. Here a fine Schefflera actinophylla *(Queensland umbrella, octopus tree) stretches upward to the skylight. Design: John Cullen.*

High rider
A glorious Nicodemia diversifolia *(indoor oak) crests a wire and aluminum utility shelf and gets its light from overhead ceiling bulbs and skylight.*

Cats and cuttings
Hedera helix *(English (ivy) and* Cissus rhombifolia *(grape ivy) cuttings share an antique bottle under the watchful gaze of two handcrafted ceramic felines.*

Baker's delight
Frequenting so many kitchens these days are French baker's racks—stunning, decorative, and, more times than not, laden with potted plants rather than pies and cakes. Here, top to bottom, are two Asparagus densiflorus 'Sprengeri' *(Sprenger asparagus), impatiens, miniature sweet William, and* Tolmiea menziesii *(piggyback). Other greenery includes a* Tripogandra multiflora *(bridal veil) by the counter and a Sprenger asparagus atop the cabinet. Design: Woodward Interiors.*

Baths

Bathing in the midst of flourishing plant life—that's a luxury the bathroom's high humidity usually allows, even in a windowless bathroom. Since the bath is likely to be the most humid room in the house, choose moisture lovers such as devil's ivy, English ivy, arrowhead vine, hollyfern, and baby's tears . . . and of course avoid plants such as cacti that require dry conditions.

Where light is a problem, you can consider rotating plants periodically to sunnier realms, or you can make the most of the easy availability and installation of artificial lights; see "Plants & Light" on pages 32—33 for more information.

Faucet flora
Bathrooms abound in nooks and crannies, making cozy habitats for small plants. Here a space behind a bright brass faucet accommodates the moisture-loving sedum. *Design: Rela Gleason.*

Something fishy
This sponge fish doesn't swim; nevertheless, it makes a big splash in a child's bathroom when used as a pot cover for Ficus pumila *(creeping fig).* Design: Rela Gleason.

Almost alfresco
The greenery surrounding a young bather echoes the lushness of growth in an outside atrium. Left to right around the tub are Dieffenbachia maculata *(dumb cane),* Maranta leuconeura *(prayer plant),* Asparagus setaceus *(fern asparagus),* tulips, Chlorophytum comosum *(spider plant), and another* Dieffenbachia maculata. *Hanging is* Nephrolepis exaltata 'Bostoniensis' *(Boston fern). Design: Sherri Waldman.*

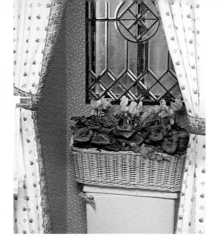

Daintily dramatic
Pots of pink and white cyclamen in a rectangular wicker basket make a ravishing temporary display on an ordinary tank top.

Perfectly pure
An all-white, old-fashioned bathroom maintains its spanking, bleached look with a grand special-occasion display of hydrangeas.

Platform for greenery
An antique mahogany back mantel is befriended by a grand assortment of green plants that are in cheery contrast to the reds of towels and wallpaper. From left are Coffea arabica *(coffee) sharing a pot with* avocado, *two* Aglaonema modestum *(Chinese evergreens),* Chlorophytum comosum *(spider plant), sweet potato,* Dieffenbachia maculata *(dumb cane),* Asparagus densiflorus 'Sprengeri' *(Sprenger asparagus), and the small-leafed* Hedera helix 'Sweetheart' *(Sweetheart ivy). Design: John Cullen.*

Plants & Windows

Plants and windows make a happy combination . . . windows providing the light that plants need to grow, and plants making a living curtain to screen unpleasant views, create privacy, and above all, fill or frame a window in a profoundly beautiful and natural way. Windows are excellent places for hanging plants (see pages 22–25), but consider other treatments, too, such as extending a window sill with a bracketed shelf or fitting several glass or wooden shelves across a window to hold small plants. Temperatures are more extreme near a window. Move plants away on very hot or cold days, and avoid direct drafts that can damage tender plants.

A place for repose
Complementary shades of blue bathe a sunny room in mellowness. Like red butterflies, the flowers of a Columnea add a flirtatious flash of color. Design: Joan Thompson.

Nocturnal drama
A bulbous pink hydrangea, an outdoor plant brought inside for a special touch of seasonal color, accentuates the color and curves of a Ming lamp and a pleasing collection of decorative pieces on a corner table. Just outside, the delicate lavender tendrils of wisteria romanticize the setting. Design: Esther Reilly.

Perfect partnership
Pelargonium peltatum (*ivy geranium*)
*and its wrought-iron stand appear to have
been made for each other. A sun lover, the
geranium gets a turn every few days for
thorough baskings and even growth.
Design: Fred and Bobbie Kleinman.*

Through the looking glass
Howea forsterana (*paradise palms*) *placed in matching wicker baskets give balance
and privacy to a uniquely low window. The* Cissus rhombifolia (*grape ivy*)*, azalea,
and curly-lashed ceramic duck add form, color—and whimsy. Design: Esther Reilly.*

Decorating Ideas **47**

...Plants & Windows

Window on the world
What better, more visible perch for a magnificent Euphorbia tirucalli (pencil tree) than a front window of smoked glass. The stark lines of this specimen plant provide an excellent contrast to the free-flowing wisteria.

High exposure, high impact
A fetching trail of Clerodendrum thomsoniae (bleeding heart glorybower) was trained to climb great heights above its floor-bound clay pot. Below, baskets of Saintpaulia ionantha (African violet) and a Nephrolepis exaltata 'Fluffy Ruffles' (fluffy ruffles fern) create a look of harmony and symmetry. Design: Susan Mueller.

Windowbox simplicity
With a layer of pebbles for drainage, fibrous begonias were planted directly into the window box and placed on a favorite kitchen sill for prominence and easy care.

City hideaway
Far above city streets, an elegantly tailored study is a perfect haven for plants such as the bright
pink-flowering Sinningia speciosa *(gloxinia),* Paphiopedilum *(lady's slipper), and the large,*
window-framing Dracaena deremensis. *Design: William Gaylord and Francis Gibbons.*
Horticultural design: Baruch Himmelstein.

...Plants & Windows

Tipping the scale
A turn-of-the-century brass and cast-iron scale gives special drama to viny plants, such as the Epipremnum aureum *(pothos).*

Easy merger
A tiled bay window extends 3½ feet into the garden outside, blending the interior with the natural landscape. Plants are predominantly fibrous begonias and Saintpaulia ionantha *(African violets), with a vibrant red* Pelargonium domesticum *(geranium) taking charge.*

Table Tops

Highlight a coffee table, chest, counter, or any other surface that could glow with the addition of a potted plant or two. Plants make handsome foils for other table-top decorations—photographs, figurines, baskets, lamps. It's usually best to select a plant that can settle down and live successfully on the available natural light.

When watering, protect wooden surfaces by taking the plant to the sink and letting moisture drain away before returning the plant to the table. You can further protect surfaces with waterproof saucers and spacers; for more about this, see "Containers," pages 14–19.

Back from the desert
Mature Echinocactus grusonii *(golden barrel cacti) are right at home in a simple, understated setting. The earthiness of the clay pots and the stark clean lines of the glass-top table complement the prickly globe-shaped plants.*

Simple and striking
Complementary earth tones, textures, and shapes make a becoming stage for this supersize anthurium. *Adding lightness to the scene is a colorful bouquet of mixed flowers atop a fossilized stone table. Design: Michael Taylor.*

...Table Tops

Teak for two

A carved Chinese teak chest plays marvelous host to two popular house plants: Saintpaulia ionantha *(African violet) and* Tolmiea menziesii *(piggy-back).*

What's cooking?

Long abandoned as a Japanese hibachi, this antique piece houses a favorite indoor plant—Nephrolepis exaltata 'Bostoniensis' (Boston fern). The hibachi's well permits an unusual view of a plant that often hangs high.

Colonial charm

Fine old pewter and a basket of mixed Saintpaulia ionantha (African violet) mean nonstop, easy charm. The violets' velvety gray green leaves complement the pewter's matte finish. Design: Susan Mueller.

A blue mood

Like clouds in an azure sky, a fragile spray of Phalaenopsis (moth orchid) beckons admirers for a lingering look. Gracefully arching over a Japanese Imari plate, it sits on a 19th century Tansu chest.

Boldly beautiful
*Gracing a fine dark oak coffee table is a
Beaucarnea recurvata (ponytail,
bottle palm). The glass container is
in two sections, allowing for drainage.
Design: Charles Falls.*

An air of importance
*With its clay pot nesting in a decorative
ceramic soup tureen, Chlorophytum
comosum (spider plant) takes a grand
position on a bamboo washstand. Green
and white tiles on the splashback repeat
the spider's variegated streaks.
Design: Fred and Bobbie Kleinman.*

Sylvan vignette
One pretty Saintpaulia ionantha *(African violet) is something to behold. Place several in a planter and you make magic. Add Pan and the fox, and you make a story. Design: Joan Thompson.*

Nostalgia in the round
A handsome Tripogandra multiflora *(bridal veil) is as much at home hanging in a pot or basket as it is here, giving height and emphasis to a family photo collection.*

Fireplaces

A focal point of any room, the fireplace makes a fine display spot for plants, whether on the mantel or on the hearth when the fireplace isn't in use. The light level is often low, though, so you should choose plants accordingly (see the Plant Selection Guide on pages 74–79). Or you can play musical pots, bringing in your most handsome bloomers to be admired, and returning them to garden or greenhouse when they begin to show signs of ennui. When your fireplace is in use, be sure nearby plants are far enough away from the fire to prevent heat damage.

Giant meets giant
A floor-to-ceiling fireplace warrants a good-size plant for company. Mood and balance require that the stone giant be paired with a plant such as the mature Beaucarnea recurvata *(ponytail, bottle palm). Horticultural design: Baruch Himmelstein.*

Welcoming spring
A host of daffodils with a fire all their own nestle—pots and all—in a basketful of inexpensive packing straw. Kept watered, the plants will stay vibrant for 2 weeks or longer.

Mantel elegance
Set the mood with candlelight and the glossy green beauty of Epipremnum aureum *(pothos). This plant makes an excellent trailer for pots and window boxes and a nice addition to large terrariums.*

Lush wagonload
An unused-in-summer fireplace needn't go unnoticed. For special occasions, roll in an antique wagon laden with annuals in bloom. Here, impatiens, an outdoor plant, was placed in a pebble-lined container of heavy-duty foil; sphagnum moss covers the soil. Design: Rela Gleason.

A study in color
Kalanchoe blossfeldiana, *a popular Christmas gift plant, is perfectly suited to the monochromatic tones of this room. It cheers a hearth in winter and will bloom again in early spring. Other varieties have yellow and pink flowers. Design: Michael Taylor.*

Plants with Art

Plants—art forms themselves—relate to, enhance, and are enhanced by other art forms. For instance, if you have two or three pots of amaryllis in bloom, placing them on a simple reed stool and adding a carved wood frog from Thailand makes the scene a source of increased delight. Try to match moods—ferns for paintings of woodsy scenes, orchids for delicate Oriental paintings, cacti for desert art. Choose plants that repeat shape or color in an art object, and the plant becomes a living extension of the artist's work.

To prevent damage to art treasures, always water and mist plants away from the area. If natural light is a threat to the art, consider artificial lighting (see pages 32—33) or rotate the plants.

Defining moods
Running, leaping deer . . . reclining, watchful deer . . . and a beautiful Aeschynanthus radicans *(lipstick plant) that creates a forest, defines a mood, makes the entire scene work as a unit. Design: Francene Markle, Sherron L. Bishop.*

Spanish primitive
Resembling a crude sled, this pebble-studded sculpture was once used as a Spanish grain thresher. Its greenmate is a Yucca gloriosa *(Spanish dagger), a rewarding choice for its immensity, shape, and lush color. Design: Michael Taylor.*

Where plants accent art
Subtly, the pink blooms of a tuberous begonia accent a poster signed by Klaes Olden-burg. Mainly an outdoor plant, the begonia divides its time between here and a patio. Design: Susan Mueller.

Green offering
The raven-haired beauty is clearly a lover of plants . . . at her feet is a Pilea num-mulariifolia *(creeping Charlie—one of several plants so named). The decorative blue stand matches her skirt and extends the mood of the painting beyond the canvas.*

Looking at scale and balance
This colorful 18th century French country clock is the focal point of an antique-filled dining room. The neighboring Cissus antarctica *(kangaroo treebine) not only picks up the leaf motif on the clock, but its height and fullness lend scale and balance to the setting. Design: John Cullen.*

Plants as Sculpture

Statuesque plants can be singled out in any crowd. These are the awe-inspiring individuals that can stand alone by virtue of their exuberant shapes. Size makes no difference . . . a svelte little 12-inch orchid plant can be just as striking as a bold old 6-foot cactus. Crafted by nature's hand, these sculptures are best displayed against plain backgrounds to enhance every shapely detail.

That one big specimen plant
Of near-human proportion, this shapely Euphorbia ingens is a living, growing (but ever so slowly) sculpture, magnificent in a contemporary room with sunny exposure. Set off alone, it holds a significance surpassing that of a dozen smaller plants. Horticultural design: Baruch Himmelstein.

A masterpiece in green
The sculptural aspects of this stunning Agave attenuata put it in the realm of nature's great works. A natural and fitting display stand is a fossilized stone mantel on a cedar stump. Design: Michael Taylor.

Reaching for the sky

The mature Dracaena marginata *is a favorite with decorators because of its exotic growth habit and dramatic appearance. It needs plenty of space, as the high-angled ceiling of this room allows. Design: Charles Falls.*

Like streaks of lightning

This tiny Oncidium sphacelatum *possesses a near-kinetic energy. The orchid's flowered streaks of lightning adorn and give importance to an otherwise plain corner. Design: Tosca Schalberg.*

A play of relationships

Here's a successful grouping of very different plants—two Ficus lyrata *(fiddleleaf figs) and a* Sansevieria trifasciata *(bowstring hemp, snake plant). The fiddleshaped and bladelike leaves make an unusual and pretty combination. Design: John Cullen.*

Decorating Ideas **61**

Plants as Centerpieces

For a very pleasing and somewhat more permanent alternative to cut flowers, consider a centerpiece of blooming plants that normally grow outdoors. A pretty pot of cyclamen, impatiens, or daffodils can blossom for weeks if it has the right care. Give your plant proper water and light, put it in a cool place overnight, and you will be amazed at its staying power. Be concerned for your table's surface—waterproof containers are safest, but a lining of plastic or foil may make other containers safe to use, at least temporarily.

In selecting your centerpiece, avoid any plant that would thwart conversation by hiding faces.

Each to his own viola
Say "welcome" with individual dinner favors that guests can take home. Here, spritely little violas are borrowed from the garden and planted in plastic-lined straw boxes whose color complements place mats and plates.

Ethereal elegance
Coming from the land of enchantment, a basket of cyclamen graces a table set for a dinner party. The plants were grown out-doors and transplanted into the aluminum-foil-lined container. If placed outside at night (moderate climate), the cyclamen can retain their freshness for as long as 2 months.

Set for casual dining
An abundance of white Sinningia
speciosa *(gloxinias) lend themselves to a
pristine country-style table setting. The
basket is large enough to accommodate
four pots of flowers, but not so big a centerpiece as to block the view of diners.
Design: Michael Taylor.*

Ready for Easter
*A batch of crocuses—double-potted and covered with sphagnum moss—is paired
with untinted Easter eggs to make a cheery seasonal centerpiece. Imaginatively com-
pleting the mood is a fanciful, gingham-ribboned rabbit, along with place mats and
candles that complement the vivid purple of the flowers.*

Decorating Ideas **63**

Basic
Plant Care

ngredients for healthy plant life
ike any working unit—either living or
echanical—a plant needs proper mainte-
ance to function normally. Shown at left
re some of the items needed to keep your
ants looking their best.

Your plants are living accessories, requiring the tender loving care that comes from a knowledge of their everyday needs. This how-to section of *Decorating with Indoor Plants* provides that knowledge and tells you how to maintain healthy house plants. It tells you how to inspect plants for possible problems, and it explains in detail the need for watering, misting, fertilizing, and repotting. Such consistent and careful attention to your plants' needs will help them thrive in their indoor environment.

Plant watching

Inspecting your house plants on a day-to-day basis or at regular intervals is a habit worth developing. Just a few minutes a day will keep them in peak condition.

Ask yourself several questions during the routine check: Does the plant need watering? Has dust accumulated on the leaves? Are any brown or dying leaves visible? Is there any sign of a pest infestation? If the answer to any of these questions is "Yes," see the appropriate section in this chapter for a solution to the problem.

Watering frequency. Plants require varying amounts of water. Some like to be constantly moist; others prefer to dry out between waterings. Know your plant's water preference; the "Plant Selection Guide" on pages 74–79 includes watering information for many house plants.

Dust accumulation. Plants, like furniture, benefit from regular dusting. Wash dirty leaves individually with plain water on a soft cloth or cotton. Always support a leaf with one hand and gently wipe off dust with the other.

Some plant lovers recommend occasional showers for their plants. You can use a spray attachment in the sink, a hose with a sprayer in the yard, or even the bathroom shower. If your home is equipped with a water softener, spray the plant outdoors with a hose, since water from outdoor faucets usually by-passes the water softener. Be sure to let plants drip dry before returning them to their normal places. And remember to limit outdoor excursions for tender house plants to the warmer seasons of the year.

Brown or dying leaves. Keep your house plants looking fresh and healthy by removing unsightly leaves. Dead or dying leaves ruin a plant's appearance and invite unwanted pests or disease. Removing dead leaves or branches also makes room for new growth.

Many leaves develop brown tips or edges (the causes are discussed on page 72). Some indoor gardeners recommend trimming these unsightly edges to keep up appearances. Use sharp scissors for this, and try to follow the natural leaf shape so the trim isn't obvious. Of course, this trimming won't correct the problem; it merely improves the plant's looks.

Pests. Most pests that attack house plants are small and hard to see. Your first indication of a problem will probably be poor plant health, which shows up as yellow or dying foliage. Examine sickly plants closely. If pests seem to be the culprit, refer to the section on their control (page 73) for a solution.

How to water wisely

Proper watering is perhaps the most important service you can give your house plants. More plants fail from improper watering than from any other cause. The best way to avoid overwatering —the most common watering offense—is to know each plant's watering needs.

"How much water?" is the first question most people ask when acquiring a plant. Many indoor plant specialists will respond evasively. Typical answers are "As much as it needs"; "Not too much, not too little"; and the all-time favorite, "It depends." Watering is indeed a very individual matter. How much and how often you water a plant will depend on the nature of the plant and the environment in which it grows.

...*Basic Plant Care*

Factors that affect watering

Since no two plants use water at exactly the same rate, there are factors beyond your control that affect the amount of water your plant needs. But you *can* control some factors, such as the type of container you select, and use them to your plant's advantage.

The seasons. In winter, when days are short and skies often gray, house plants generally need less water than during the summertime. Some plants respond to winter by retreating into a state of listlessness. They don't require much water; instead, give them dry aid and comfort by continuing your routine inspections and making sure they have adequate light. When your listless plant perks up, resume its normal care.

Plant dormancy. Some plants have a season for going completely dormant. The foliage of most tuberous and bulbous plants (the plants most likely to have dormant periods) begins to yellow after the plants bloom. Gradually withhold water from these plants until the foliage is dry. Then store the pots with the tubers or bulbs in a cool, dry, out-of-the-way spot. When new growth appears, restore the plant to its customary place.

Containers. The container you choose to hold your plant will affect the amount of water needed and how often you apply it. Plant containers and their influence on watering are discussed in more detail on pages 15–18.

Plant differences. Plants that grow quickly and those that bloom or bear fruit heavily need more water than plants with a more conservative life style. Plants with a large total leaf surface, such as ferns, require more water than sparsely foliaged plants. Plants with soft, lush foliage need more water than those with waxy, leathery, or succulent leaves.

A good way to water

Let's assume your plant has the proper potting mix and drainage (see "Filling the pot," page 68, and "Step-by-step potting," page 69). You should then feel the top inch of the soil. If it is dry to the touch, add tepid water to the soil surface. Continue to add water until you see it seeping from the drainage hole. Allow the plant to drain (either into a sink or drainage tray) for a minimum of 10 minutes. Discard any excess water standing in the tray—a potted plant should never sit in water. Repeat this procedure when the soil surface again is dry to the touch.

Use a watering can with a straight or slightly curved spout. This prevents you from spilling as you water.

After you have followed this watering procedure for a time, you should be able to estimate the amount of water your plants utilize. Add the amount of water each plant uses; then, in a few minutes, check the drainage trays for any excess water.

The soak

Many kinds of house plants, especially Boston ferns, benefit from occasionally having their entire pots totally immersed in water. Soak the pot (have water at room temperature) until bubbles stop coming to the surface. Remove the plant, let it drain, and then return it to its normal location. This is a good time—immediately after a periodic dunking—to apply fertilizer. (Fertilizing is discussed on pages 67–68.)

The humidity factor

Most home atmospheres contain a negligible amount of humidity. This lack of moisture in the air is no problem for a few plant families, such as cactus and succulents, but the majority of plants we try to grow indoors originated in tropical jungles, dripping with natural moisture. While a "rain forest" environment is hardly desirable for our homes, some humidity is essential to our house plants. It is helpful, then, to understand the many factors affecting the humidity level inside a house.

During the winter months, heating systems reduce natural humidity. Warm summer temperatures also evaporate most moisture. The humidity levels in your home can be gauged by a hygrometer, an instrument that measures the amount of moisture present in the air. Inexpensive hygrometers are usually available in hardware stores.

Several methods allow you to increase humidity for your plants: misting, utilizing humidity trays, grouping compatible plants, and placing plants in naturally humid areas.

Daily misting is an easy, inexpensive method of creating a humid atmosphere for your tropical plants. Opinions vary among indoor gardeners on the value of misting plants. Daily misting is popular among many orchid and fern lovers; other gardeners mist only occasionally or not at all. Besides creating humidity, misting has the added advantage of cleaning foliage and discouraging pests.

Misting should create a fine spray of moisture that surrounds your plant and covers both sides of its leaves. Like watering, misting should be done in the morning so the moisture will have time to evaporate. It's best to let water sit in the mister overnight; this allows the chlorine to dissipate. Keep in mind, though, that misting does not replace regular watering since the plant absorbs very little of the spray.

Some hairy-leafed plants, such as African violets, dislike being misted. Water drops on the leaves may cause spotting, especially if the water is below room temperature.

Plastic and metal misters are available in most nurseries and garden centers. Be sure your mister sprays a fine mist. The plant leaves should not be dripping wet; they should look as if a light dew has settled on them.

Humidity trays provide for constant water evaporation around house plants. Waterproof trays, large enough to hold one plant or several, are filled with small rocks or pebbles. Add enough water to the tray so the water level remains just below the top of the rocks. The plant container rests on the rocks, preventing it from ever sitting in water (roots that are constantly immersed in water may rot). This tray will also catch any runoff created during regular watering.

Trays should be constructed of waterproof materials, such as metal, plastic, nonabsorbent rubber, or glazed ceramic.

Grouping compatible plants is another method of creating humidity indoors. All plants give off water vapor through their leaves in a process called transpiration. This water vapor creates humidity around each transpiring plant. And besides creating moisture for each other, a group of plants is always more interesting visually than the single parlor palm standing forlornly in a corner.

Naturally humid areas in most homes are the kitchen and the bathroom. The normal activities performed in these rooms, such as washing dishes, boiling water, or taking hot showers, generate moisture and frequently raise the humidity level.

Moisture-loving plants will thrive in these rooms if their other requirements, such as light and temperature, can also be met.

Fertilizing know-how

Many people think that fertilizer is food for their plants. This is not precisely true. Plants manufacture their own food by the process of photosynthesis. The fertilizers you provide your house plants assist them in this food production. In short, you're helping your plants feed themselves. Most gardeners, however, use the terms "fertilizing" and "feeding" interchangeably.

Plants living in the ground outdoors can search for the nutrients they need. If their immediate area lacks these needed nutrients, their roots can branch into other areas. A house plant, on the other hand, is confined to the soil in its pot; once the nutrients in the potting mix are gone, the plant is stranded. But you can replenish these nutrients by applying fertilizer.

House plant fertilizers usually contain three main nutrients: nitrogen, phosphorus, and potassium or potash. Some fertilizers also include needed trace elements. The ratio of these three ingredients is usually indicated on the label by three numbers, such as 5-10-5 or 18-20-16. The first number refers to nitrogen, which stimulates leaf growth and helps leaves maintain a rich green color. The second number indicates phosphorus, which promotes sturdy cell structure and healthy root growth and aids in flower and fruit production. The third number refers to potassium, which aids plants in normal plant functions and development. If you choose a fertilizer that indicates it is formulated for house plants, you can feel confident it is properly balanced in the three main nutrients.

Types of fertilizers

Commercial fertilizers for house plants come in several forms: liquid, powder, tablet, and capsule. Most of these fertilizers are dissolved and diluted

Two types of humidity trays you can create: individual saucer filled with small pebbles (left) holds
plant so drained-off water never touches pot; large tray (right) provides humidity for group of house plants.

in water for application. Some are scratched into the soil surface, others are placed on the soil surface or in the soil. The slow-release fertilizers allow nutrients to be dissolved in normal waterings over a period of time.

Using fertilizers wisely

Whichever type of house plant fertilizer you choose, read the label carefully and follow the directions exactly. Too much fertilizer can burn or even kill an otherwise healthy plant, and fertilizer applied at the wrong time can also hurt a plant. That is why experienced plant lovers never apply fertilizer to dry potting mix. They thoroughly water their plants first. Knowing it's unwise to force a sick plant to grow, they never fertilize an ailing plant, either. Instead, they wait until it has completely recovered before encouraging it to grow.

Most plants rest during the winter months, so don't coax them into growth by applying fertilizer; wait until they show signs of growth. Most gardeners avoid fertilizers from about September to March.

A newly purchased house plant normally will have been well nourished at the nursery or greenhouse and won't need fertilizer, either, for at least 3 months. A newly repotted plant will find sufficient nutrients in the new potting mix and won't need fertilizer for a while.

"An extra pinch to grow on" can damage a plant severely. If you find you have applied too much fertilizer, leaching your plant may wash out some of the excess. (Leaching means watering your plant so water comes out the drainage hole, letting it drain for a while, and then rewatering. This process is repeated two or three times.)

Many indoor gardeners, however, find it very beneficial to apply fertilizers more often (usually twice as often) than is recommended on fertilizer labels—but in a very diluted state (usually one-half the recommended dose or less). This provides the plant with nutrients in a more consistent manner.

Filling the pot

Potting mix is the all-important ingredient for healthy plants. It forms the medium in which plants live and grow; it provides the initial nutrients plants need; and it permits moisture retention while allowing any excess water to drain away.

Commercial potting mixes

For most indoor gardeners, buying a package of prepared potting mix is the most efficient method of selecting house plant soil. Potting mix is sold in various quantities, so you can purchase only the amount you need at the time. If you have any left over, simply reseal it in its package for later use.

Buy a commercial mix specifically formulated for house plants; it temporarily provides the nutrients that plants need. When it becomes necessary, you can replenish these nutrients with a house plant fertilizer (see pages 67–68). The packaged potting mix has been sterilized to eliminate any pests or diseases that might be present. Such mixes are readily available at nurseries, indoor plant stores, or other stores where garden supplies are sold.

Some lightweight mixes need to be moistened before planting. Squeeze a handful of soil in your fist; the mix should be damp enough to form a compact ball when you release it, yet not be dripping wet. If the mix is dry and crumbly, add enough water to the mix to make it cohesive.

If you want to make your own

If you're a purist, and purchasing a commercial potting mix in a plastic bag isn't your idea of going back to the earth, you can make your own potting mix. Just blend equal amounts of coarse sand, garden loam or good garden topsoil, and peat moss, leaf mold, or fir bark. (Be sure to buy washed sand; the salt in unwashed sea sand may damage tender plants.) To *each* 2 quarts of this mix, add ½ cup *each* charcoal and perlite.

Every ingredient in your potting mix has a purpose. Garden loam or topsoil contains particles of clay that hold fertilizing materials in an available state for plant roots to absorb. Sand, perlite, and leaf mold hold air around the roots, which is essential to good plant growth. Leaf mold also provides some nutrients. Charcoal bits keep the soil "sweet" by absorbing any noxious by-products created in decaying matter in the soil or potting mix. All of these ingredients are usually available at most nurseries, garden supply stores, and indoor plant stores.

Any potting mix that you make yourself which contains garden soil must be sterilized. Garden loam or topsoil may contain pests, weed seeds, or plant diseases; sterilizing the mix eliminates these problems.

Follow these steps to sterilize your soil: Mix all ingredients thoroughly; slightly dampen the mix with water; then spread it —no more than 4 inches deep— in shallow ovenproof pans. Place the filled pans in a 180° oven and bake for at least 2 hours.

Be prepared for the nasty odor of baking soil; luckily, this odor isn't lasting. Remove the sterilized soil from the oven and let it air for a few days. Then store it in sturdy paper or plastic bags.

Step-by-step potting

Potting brings it all together: your house plant, its container, and the potting mix in which it will live. Before you begin, have all the necessary materials ready and waiting; finding yourself out of potting mix with the container half filled is frustrating.

Work in an easy-to-clean area; transplanting is a messy business. And work quickly to avoid shock to the plant. If you are interrupted, cover the exposed root ball with damp towels and return to the transplanting as soon as possible.

Planting procedures

Once you've gathered together your house plant, potting mix, cleaned container, and any other needed materials, you can begin transplanting.

• Remove the plant from its present container, keeping the root ball intact. If the plant refuses to budge from its pot, brace the stem and soil surface with one hand and invert the pot with the other. Strike the pot rim carefully against a solid surface, such as a table top or counter; this should loosen the root ball and allow it to emerge in one piece. If this doesn't dislodge the plant, run a sharp knife between the pot and the root ball and invert the pot.

• Place pot shards (curved, broken bits of old clay pots) or pebbles over the drainage hole. This prevents the potting mix from draining out of the pot when the plant is watered. If you use pot shards, place them over the drainage hole as shown in illustration 2 on page 70. If you use pebbles, be sure they don't completely plug the drainage hole.

• Put enough potting mix in the bottom of the pot so that the top surface of the root ball, when placed in the pot, will be about ½ inch below the container rim. This level works best for watering plants (see illustration 3). In larger pots, you may want to leave more than ½ inch at the top to keep things in proportion.

• Center the root ball in the container and fill in the sides with potting mix. Occasionally, thump the container on your working surface to settle in the new soil (see illustrations 4 and 5). Continue to add potting mix until the sides are just level with the root ball surface. Be careful not to bury the root ball any deeper —plants can suffocate.

• Smooth out the surface of the new potting mix with your fingers. Don't push down the root ball or the plant stem; this could damage fragile hair roots.

• Water your newly potted plant thoroughly; then step back and admire. Once your plant resumes its normal appearance and vitality, you can assume it has adjusted to its new container, and move it to its permanent location. At this point, resume normal care of your plant.

1. Remove plant and root ball intact from original container.

2. Cover drainage hole with pebbles or pot shards; add some potting mix.

3. Make soil layer deep enough to lift root ball almost to pot rim.

4. Center root ball and steady it as you fill insides with potting mix.

5. Thump pot carefully on working surface to settle potting mix.

6. Smooth soil surface gently with fingers, avoiding plant stem area.

Growing in a drainless container

Growing a house plant in a container without a drainage hole isn't ideal, but it can be done. Problems arise when the plant is watered, because once in, the water has no escape. The solution is to provide a drainage layer inside the container to act as a holding tank for the excess moisture.

Place a layer of small rocks or pebbles in the bottom of the container. This layer should take up about one quarter of the total container volume. (You can also use small pieces of lava or "feather rock" or broken bits of clay pots for the drainage material.) The drainage layer allows water to seep through the soil and retains it until the moisture can be utilized by the plant—or until the moisture evaporates. Another advantage of the drainage layer is that it keeps the plant roots from sitting in soggy soil and permits the roots to obtain oxygen.

Next, spread a thin layer of charcoal bits directly over the drainage layer. As mentioned before, charcoal keeps the soil "sweet" by absorbing any noxious by-products created in decaying matter in the soil or potting mix.

Begin putting in the potting mix and proceed with the transplanting as described on pages 69–70. The various layers used in a drainless container are shown on page 71.

The adjustment period

Adjusting to a new container can be traumatic for a plant. It usually needs a respite before being placed in its permanent location.

Place the newly potted and well-watered plant in a cool, sunless spot for several days. (A sun-loving plant is an exception; place it immediately in its permanent location.) If it wilts, don't rewater it unless the potting mix is bone dry at least an inch below the surface. Instead, try misting to rejuvenate the plant, or create a greenhouse atmosphere by sealing the plant—pot and all—in a plastic bag.

Once it has adjusted to potting, move your plant to its permanent location.

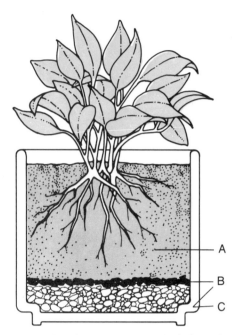

Soil layers inside a drainless container include potting mix (A), charcoal (B), drainage material (C).

Pinching for size, pruning for shape

Plant size is an important consideration indoors. Limitations such as ceilings, table tops, and room size indicate the optimal size for your house plants, but how do you keep plants to scale? Careful pinching and pruning is the solution. Pinching encourages bushy growth; pruning reshapes an overgrown plant. Root pruning, though somewhat more drastic, can increase the indoor life of a favorite plant.

Tools for trimming

Though the average gardener requires a wide variety of pruning tools in all shapes and sizes, the indoor gardener needs only a few. The two most generally useful pruning tools are your thumb and forefinger —these tools you'll never misplace. They can handle most pruning on soft-stemmed plants. Have a sharp knife, scissors, or hand pruners for tougher jobs.

Pinching

Like preventive medicine, proper use of the pinching technique avoids more drastic pruning measures. Pinching out the growing tip of a stem promotes side branching that creates thick, bushy plants; pinching stops growth in one direction and redirects it.

Using your thumb and forefinger, pinch out the top growth of a stem or branch. This forces side buds lower on the stem to form new branches. The resulting growth helps create a full, well-shaped plant and keeps it from becoming leggy. Tip pinching is shown on page 72.

Pinching should be used on fast-growing, branching plants —such as Swedish ivy, wandering Jew, or coleus—that can form new growth on pinched stems. Do not pinch a plant with a single growing stem, such as a dracaena or palm.

Repeat pinching as often as necessary during the plant's growing season. Be sure to pinch only stems that contain at least three or four sets of leaves; these are established and can support new growth.

Top pruning

Like pinching, top pruning restores the plant's desired shape. Removing leggy growth or branches grown awry improves the plant's appearance and, as with pinching, may encourage new growth.

Cut stems or branches back to where you want them. Use scissors or pruning shears if the stem is too stiff to be pinched off with thumb and forefinger. Always cut just above a leaf node or bud. Be sure to remove as much of the stem above the node as possible. The node or bud becomes the terminal growing point on the stem, and water and nutrients will travel no farther. The dead and dying stem is useless and could become diseased, endangering your plant.

If you decide to remove a whole branch, cut it off as close to the main stem as possible.

Root pruning

If a plant has reached the maximum size your house can accommodate, consider root pruning.

(Continued on next page)

*1. **Leggy plant** needs to grow bushier, keep more compact form.*

*2. **Pinch out** growing tip of tallest stem, removing it close to leaf joint.*

*3. **New growth** forms just below pinched-out tip, makes plant bushy.*

This process takes courage but, if successful, permits your plant to remain in its present container. Root pruning techniques are illustrated on page 73.

It's best to root prune a house plant during a time of active growth, usually in the spring. Have all materials ready so the procedure can be accomplished as quickly as possible. Remove the plant from its pot and, with a sharp knife, trim off portions of the root ball on all sides. Cut quickly; do not saw or hack at roots. With plants that have fleshy roots, such as asparagus ferns, spider plants, or dracaena, severe root pruning could be detrimental; instead, wash all the old soil off the roots and then repot.

When you replace the root-pruned plant in its container, leave about 1-inch clearance on all sides. Fill in the sides with new potting mix, and tamp the plant in. Then water the plant and return it to its place.

A root-pruned plant will revive more quickly if it is also top pruned.

Common problems

This section lists plant problems and the effect each has on a plant's appearance. It offers possible causes and suggests methods for correction. Study each plant's problem carefully and try to diagnose and treat it as quickly as possible.

Leaf tips and leaf margins turn brown from improper plant care. Overwatering or underwatering, using water with a high salt concentration, too much sun or heat through a window, too much fertilizer, humidity, or locating the plant in drafts—or a combination of these care problems—may result in browned tips or margins. Study your plant's situation and try to locate the possible cause. If the cause isn't easily discernible, try eliminating each possibility, one at a time.

Yellowing leaves on house plants have a variety of possible causes. Common problems are not enough light or too much light, and lack of fertilizer or too much fertilizer. Yellowing leaves may also be the result of a high nighttime temperature or too much water. Sucking insects (probably scale insects or mealybugs) on plant stems between the yellowing leaves and the roots are another possible cause. Study the care you give your plant to locate the cause of the yellowing foliage. The green color may or may not return to the damaged leaves after the problem is corrected.

Leaf drop can be caused by overwatering or underwatering, too much sun, too much fertilizer, not enough humidity, or a drafty location. If only the lower leaves drop, your plant probably needs more light. Once leaves have fallen off because of improper care, they seldom grow back.

Wilting is a normal plant reaction to too much sun or heat, too much or too little water, or a poor growing location. Try moving the plant to a better spot and check your watering techniques. Plants that need water will perk up quickly after a needed drink. Wilting isn't detrimental to the plant as long as it isn't allowed to happen too frequently.

*1. **Remove plant** from pot. With sharp knife, slice off portions of root ball.*

*2. **Place root ball** on top of enough soil to bring plant up to pot rim.*

*3. **Top prune** to help plant recover and to improve its shape.*

Dry and brittle leaves may mean your plant isn't getting enough water or the humidity levels are too low. Review your watering practices. Try regular misting or place the plant on a humidity tray (humidity trays are discussed on page 67).

Leggy growth is caused by insufficient light. Try moving your house plant to a location with more light, and pinch back the leggy stems.

Soft stem bases on house plants usually indicate rot. Overwatering is probably the culprit. Watch your watering habits carefully.

Plant pests & diseases

There are two approaches to pest control: one is direct, involving physical removal of the pests; the other, requiring the use of pesticides, is less direct and not always beneficial to the plant.

The direct approach is to remove pests by hand or to wash them off with water from a hose or under a water faucet. Some gardeners have been successful using a mist sprayer. An advantage of this approach is that it can be repeated as often as needed to control pests whereas most insecticides require a certain waiting period between doses. The chief disadvantage of this direct method is that it doesn't eliminate insect eggs in the soil.

Spraying plants with insecticides can be almost as harmful to some house plants as the pest infestation itself. Always read and carefully follow label directions. Be sure the insecticide will effectively eliminate the specific pest attacking your plant. Also be certain that it is recommended for house plants, and for the particular plant that is infested.

It's best to spray plants outdoors. When you do, any spray residue will be dispersed outside in the open air. In addition, you can be sure to cover the leaf surfaces, both top and bottom, without worrying about damaging furniture surfaces. It's also best, for convenience and economy, to use house plant insecticides in pump or spray containers. Other types of sprays need to be mixed (a time-consuming and messy process requiring special equipment) and are available only in large quantities.

Your first step is to identify your plant problem as a pest infestation. Some pests, such as mealybugs or aphids, will be visible on the plant or in the container. Others, too small for visual identification, will be indicated only by plant symptoms or damage, such as webbing or stunted growth. Once you've detected a pest problem, isolate the infested plant immediately to prevent infestation of other plants.

It is rather uncommon for house plants to develop diseases. Most disease problems result from poor growing conditions or purchasing an already diseased plant.

Crown or root rot is usually caused by poor drainage and overwatering. Plants may turn brown or suddenly wilt. If the plant isn't too far gone, transplanting may be beneficial.

Mildew appears on plant leaves, stems, or flower buds as a white or gray powder. Leaves may curl or be distorted. Overwatering and poor air circulation are probable causes.

Plant Selection Guide

In these charts we present a listing of favorite indoor plants, along with individual plant descriptions and information on light and water needs. Under "Comments," additional care details or general notes are offered. Numbers in parentheses refer to pages where the plant is pictured.

Key to light and water needs: *Sun* indicates the plant should have sunlight for at least half the day; *Indirect* means good light exposure but no direct sun; *Low* refers to plants that can take only a small amount of sunlight. *Dry* means that the soil should become dry to the touch between waterings; *Moist,* that the soil should remain moist (but not wet) between waterings; *Wet,* that a plant requires frequent waterings or is grown in water.

Plants are listed alphabetically by their botanical names in the charts; you'll find common names in the second column.

BOTANICAL NAME	COMMON NAME	DESCRIPTION	LIGHT NEEDS	WATER NEEDS	COMMENTS*
Adiantum tenerum	Maidenhair fern	Arching, spreading growth. Long, broad, bright green fronds, finely divided into many deeply cut segments ½–¾″ wide.	Low	Moist	Needs soil rich in organic matter. (19, 30)
Aechmea fasciata	Bromeliad	Upright. Gray green leaves, cross banded with silvery white. Cluster of pink flower bracts.	Indirect	Dry	Apply water every week or two into cups within leaves. Put water on soil when it's really dry to the touch. (6)
Aeschynanthus radicans	Lipstick plant	Trailing. Tubular red flowers.	Indirect	Moist	Plant in loose, fibrous potting mix. Excellent as a hanging plant. (21, 25, 58)
Agave americana	Century plant	Upright. Blue green leaves to 2½′ long with hooked spines along the edge and a wicked spine at the tip.	Sun	Dry	There are also several varieties with yellow or white striped leaves. (30)
Agave attenuata		Clumps up to 5 feet across. Leaves soft green or gray green.	Indirect	Dry	Statuesque container plant. Protect from hot sun. (60)
Agave victoriae-reginae		6″-long dark green leaves, 2″ wide, stiff, thick with narrow white lines.	Indirect	Moist	Slow growing, it will stand in pot 20 years before flowering (greenish flowers on tall stalks), then die. (30)
Aglaonema modestum	Chinese evergreen	Upright. Leaves up to 18 inches long, 5 inches across.	Indirect	Moist	An easily grown, low-maintenance house plant. (45)
Allium tuberosum	Garlic chives	Upright, spreading growth. Clumps of gray green, flat leaves. White flowers in summer.	Sun or indirect	Moist	Leaves have mild garlic flavor, are useful in salads, cooked dishes. Dormant in winter. (14)
Anthurium		Upright. Variety of leaf shapes. Flowering.	Indirect	Wet	The higher the humidity, the better. Protect from drafts. Use diluted fertilizer every 4 weeks. (51)
Araucaria heterophylla	Norfolk Island pine	Tree. Evenly spaced tiers of stiff branches. Juvenile leaves rather narrow, ½″ long, curved with sharp point; mature leaves somewhat triangular and densely overlapping.	Indirect	Moist	Can be held in container for many years; can double as indoor Christmas tree. Likes cool temperatures, good light, standard potting mix. Don't crowd; needs good air circulation.
Arecastrum romanzoffianum	Queen palm	Tree. Exceptionally straight trunk. Bright green, glossy feathery leaves.	Indirect	Wet	Fast grower, responding quickly to water and fertilizer. Very subject to mites; wash frequently. (37)
Asparagus densiflorus 'Sprengeri'	Sprenger asparagus	Arching, trailing growth. Shiny, bright green, needlelike leaves.	Indirect	Moist	Popular for hanging baskets or containers, indoors and out. (27, 43, 45)

BOTANICAL NAME	COMMON NAME	DESCRIPTION	LIGHT NEEDS	WATER NEEDS	COMMENTS*
Asparagus setaceus	Fern asparagus	Arching, trailing growth. Tiny threadlike leaves form dark green feathery sprays.	Indirect	Moist	Dense, fine-textured foliage mass useful as screen, hanger. (41, 44)
Asplenium bulbiferum	Mother fern	Arching, upright growth. Graceful, finely cut, light green fronds.	Low	Moist	Fronds produce plantlets that can be removed and planted. (21, 38)
Beaucarnea recurvata	Ponytail Bottle palm	Succulent shrub or tree. Base of trunk is greatly swollen. Arching, drooping leaves.	Sun	Dry	Young plants touching window can freeze in cold weather. (36, 54, 56)
Begonia		Upright, arching growth. Many varieties, tuberous, rhizomatous, or fibrous-rooted.	Indirect	Moist to dry	All kinds are generally best in filtered shade with rich, porous, fast-draining, slightly acid soil, and consistent fertilizing. (30, 40, 48, 50, 59)
Caladium bicolor	Fancy-leafed caladium	Upright, arching growth. Large, arrow-shaped, long-stalked, almost translucent leaves colored in bands and blotches of red, rose, pink, white, silver, bronze, and green.	Indirect	Moist	Best adapted as summer pot plant in sheltered patios or plunged in borders. Bring indoors in cold climates. (30)
Chamaedorea elegans	Neanthe bella Parlor palm	Upright. Single-stemmed; grows very slowly to eventual 3–4'.	Indirect or low	Moist	Tolerates poor light, crowded roots. Repot every 2–3 years, carefully washing off old soil and replacing with good potting mix. (8, 30)
Chlorophytum comosum	Spider plant	Clumps of soft curving leaves like long broad grass blades. Tiny white flowers. 'Variegatum' and 'Vittatum' with white striped leaves are popular.	Indirect	Dry	Great for hanging containers and baskets. Miniature duplicates of mother plant, complete with root, can be cut off and potted individually. (6, 20, 38, 41, 44, 45, 54)
Cissus antarctica	Kangaroo treebine	Vining. Medium green shiny leaves, 2–3½" long and almost as wide. Toothed edges.	Indirect or low	Dry to moist	Excellent both for hanging and table-top display. (11, 22, 59)
Cissus rhombifolia	Grape ivy	Vining. Dark green leaves divided into diamond-shaped leaflets with sharp-toothed edges.	Indirect or low	Dry to moist	Excellent both for hanging and table-top display. (27, 35, 43, 47) Variety 'Ellen Danika' has shallowly lobed leaflets like an oak leaf; darker green, less lustrous than grape ivy. (Cover, 30)
Clerodendrum thomsoniae	Bleeding heart glorybower	Vining. Leaves oval, 4–7" long, dark green, shiny, and ribbed. Flowers are scarlet tubes surrounded by large white calyxes.	Indirect	Moist	Needs rich, loose soil mix. Prune after flowering. (48)
Coffea arabica	Coffee	Tree. Evenly spaced branches clothed with shining, dark green oval leaves. Fragrant white flowers.	Indirect	Moist	Can grow up to 15' with proper conditions. (45)
Coleus hybridus	Coleus	Upright. Leaves may be 3–6" long in large-leafed strains; 1–1½" long in newer dwarf strains. Colors include green, yellow, buff, salmon, red, purple, and brown, often with many colors on a single leaf.	Indirect	Moist	Popular hanger. Cuttings root in water as well as other rooting media. (30)
Columnea		Trailing or arching growth; sometimes shrubby. Paired, shiny leaves; flowers are long tubes with flared mouths.	Indirect	Moist	Popular hanger. There are many named varieties, all good-looking. Easiest to find is Columnea 'Stavanger' (Norse fire plant). (46)
Crassula argentea	Jade plant	Upright, spreading growth. Leaves are thick, oblong, fleshy pads 1–2" long, glossy bright green, sometimes with red-tinged edges.	Sun, indirect, or low	Dry	Likes warm temperatures, potting mix consisting of 1/2 standard potting mix, 1/2 sharp sand. Plants will stay small in small containers.
Cyclamen		Upright growth. Attractive leaves in basal clumps. Grown for pretty white, pink, rose, or red flowers that resemble shooting stars.	Indirect	Moist	Needs fairly rich, porous soil with lots of humus. (14, 30, 45, 62)

*Numbers in parentheses refer to pages where plant is pictured.

BOTANICAL NAME	COMMON NAME	DESCRIPTION	LIGHT NEEDS	WATER NEEDS	COMMENTS*
Cymbidium		Upright, arching growth. Long, narrow, grasslike foliage forms sheath around short, stout, oval pseudo-bulbs. Long-lasting flowers grow on erect or arching spikes.	Indirect	Moist (See comments)	Keep potting mix constantly moist from March through October. Needs cool nighttime temperatures (45°–55° F/7°–13° C). (28, 38)
Davallia trichomanoides	Squirrel's foot fern	Trailing, arching growth. Very finely divided fronds up to 12″ long, 6″ wide, rise from light reddish brown, furry rhizomes (like squirrel's feet).	Indirect	Moist	Best displayed as hanger. Use light, fast-draining soil mix. (30)
Dieffenbachia amoena	Dumb cane	Upright. To 6′ or higher. Broad, dark green, 18″-long leaves marked with narrow, white, slanting stripes on either side of midrib.	Indirect	Dry	Potting soil should drain freely. Fertilize bimonthly in spring and summer with half-strength liquid fertilizer. (29)
Dieffenbachia maculata (D. picta)	Dumb cane	Upright. To 6′ or higher. Wide, oval, green leaves, 10″ or more in length, have greenish white dots and patches.	Indirect	Dry	Potting soil should drain freely. Fertilize bimonthly in spring and summer with half-strength liquid fertilizer. (20, 44, 45)
Dizygotheca elegantissima	Threadleaf false aralia	Shrub. Leaves on juvenile plants are lacy—divided like fans into very narrow leaflets with notched edges. As plants mature, leaves become bigger with notched leaflets.	Indirect	Moist	Needs fast-draining, moisture-retentive soil mix. Fertilize monthly. Subject to pests indoors. (30)
Dracaena deremensis		Tree. Erect, slow growing, but eventually 15′ tall. Long, 2′ leaves are rich green, striped white and gray.	Low	Dry	In containers, water only when top ½ to 1″ of soil is dry. (22, 49)
Dracaena marginata		Tree. Slender, erect, smooth gray stems to eventual 12′. Leaves are deep glossy green.	Indirect	Dry	Very easy, very popular house plant. If it grows too tall, cut off crown and reroot it. (61)
Echinocactus grusonii	Golden barrel cactus	Upright. Slow-growing cactus to 4′ high, 2½′ in diameter, with showy yellow, stiff 3″ spines.	Indirect	Dry	Excellent table-top display plant. (51)
Epipremnum aureum (Pothos aureus, Raphidophora aurea)	Pothos	Trailing. Oval, leathery leaves 2–4″ long, bright green splashed or marbled with yellow.	Indirect	Dry to moist	Attractive trailer for pots, window boxes, large terrariums. (20, 37, 50, 57)
Euphorbia ingens		Upright growth. Leafless, cactuslike stems. Eventually tree-sized.	Sun	Dry	Slow-growing, dramatic specimen plant. (60)
Euphorbia milii (E. splendens)	Crown of thorns	Upright. Shrubby, climbing stems to 3–4′ armed with long sharp thorns. Leaves roundish, thin, light green.	Sun or indirect	Moist	Grows best in porous soil. Tolerates drought but does better with regular watering. (30)
Euphorbia tirucalli	Pencil tree	Tree or large shrub. Single or multiple trunks support tangle of light green, pencil-thick, succulent branches with no sign of a leaf.	Sun	Moist	Striking for pattern of silhouette or shadow. (48)
Ficus benjamina	Weeping Chinese banyan	Tree. Shining green, leathery, poplarlike leaves up to 5″ long.	Sun or indirect	Moist	Undoubtedly most popular indoor plant. Dislikes overwatering, dark growing conditions, drafts, heat registers, and being moved. (12–13, 21, 27, 28, 30, 34, 35, 37, 40)
Ficus carica	Edible fig	Tree. Leaves rough, bright green, 3–5 lobed, 4–9″ long and nearly as wide.	Sun	Moist	Strong trunk and branch pattern make fig a top-notched ornamental tree. (35)
Ficus deltoidea (F. diversifolia)	Mistletoe fig	Shrub. Interesting, open twisted branch pattern. Thick, dark green, roundish 2″ leaves are sparsely stippled with tan specks on upper surface.	Indirect	Moist	Most often grown in containers as patio and house plant. (14)

BOTANICAL NAME	COMMON NAME	DESCRIPTION	LIGHT NEEDS	WATER NEEDS	COMMENTS*
Ficus lyrata	Fiddleleaf fig	Tree or large shrub. Huge, dark green, fiddle-shaped leaves up to 15″ long and 10″ wide, prominently veined, with glossy surface.	Indirect	Moist	Dramatic structural form. To increase branching, pinch back when young. (33, 35, 36, 61)
Ficus pumila	Creeping fig	Vining. Neat little leaves of juvenile growth ultimately develop into large, leathery, oblong leaves borne on stubby branches.	Indirect	Moist	Usually grown outdoors as climber. Attractive foliage for container display. (44)
Ficus rubiginosa	Rustyleaf fig	Tree. Dense foliage of 5″ oval leaves, deep green above and generally rusty, woolly beneath.	Indirect or sun	Moist	Excellent as room divider or corner tree. (28)
Hedera helix	English ivy	Vining. Leaves are dark, dull green with paler veins, 3–5 lobed, 2–4″ wide at base and as long.	Indirect or sun	Moist	Neat and dependable house plant, ground cover. Good table-top display or hanger. (6, 19, 30, 40, 43, 45)
Howea forsterana	Paradise palm	Tree. Leaves up to 9′ long, with long drooping leaflets. Green trunk ringed with leaf scars.	Indirect	Moist	Howeas (sometimes called kentias) are the classic parlor palms. Keep fronds clean and dust-free to minimize spider mite problem. (Cover, 8, 47)
Hoya carnosa	Wax flower Wax plant	Vining. Has 2–4″-long oval leaves; big, round, tight clusters of creamy white flowers ½″ across.	Sun	Dry	Blooms best when potbound; usually grown in containers, even outdoors. (42)
Kalanchoe blossfeldiana		Upright. Leaves fleshy, dark green edged with red. Shiny, smooth edged or slightly lobed. Small bright flower in big clusters held above leaves.	Sun or indirect	Dry	Popular house plant at Christmas time. (30, 57)
Lindernia grandiflora	Blue angel tears	Sprawling, spreading, or trailing growth. Pairs of roundish, bright green, ½″ leaves. Tiny flowers look pale blue but are actually white with purple stripes.	Indirect or low	Moist	Needs rich soil and occasional fertilizing. (6)
Livistona chinensis	Chinese fountain palm	Tree. Outer edges of 3–6′ roundish, bright green leaves droop markedly.	Indirect or sun	Moist	These palms are self-cleaning (no pruning of old leaves needed); trunk is leaf-scarred. (9, 39)
Maranta leuconeura	Prayer plant	Upright. Leaves 7–8″ long and half as wide, short stalked, becoming whitish along midrib and veins; brown spots toward margin.	Indirect	Moist	Must have warmth, occasional trimming, lots of water, and regular fertilizing (fish emulsion is good) to be at its best. (30, 44)
Monstera deliciosa	Split-leaf philodendron	Upright growth. Leaves on youngest plants uncut; mature leaves heavy, leathery, dark green, deeply cut and perforated.	Indirect or low	Moist	For best results indoors, grow in container with good drainage, feed occasionally, and keep leaves clean.
Neoregelia		Upright, arching growth. Bromeliads with rosettes of leathery leaves, often strikingly colored or marked, and with short spikes of usually inconspicuous flowers.	Indirect	Moist	Feed lightly. Keep water in cup at base of rosette. Needs light, open, fast-draining planting mix that holds moisture. (33)
Nephrolepis exaltata 'Bostoniensis'	Boston fern	Spreading, arching growth. Graceful, eventually drooping fronds.	Indirect	Dry	Classic parlor fern of grandmother's day. Fertilize every month with diluted liquid fertilizer. Among more finely cut and feathery forms, 'Fluffy Ruffles', 'Rooseveltii', and 'Whitmanii' are the best known. (30, 41, 44, 53)
Nephrolepis exaltata 'Fluffy Ruffles'	Fluffy ruffles fern	Upright, arching growth. Tall (to 5′), with fronds up to 6″ wide.	Indirect	Dry	Tough, easy-to-grow fern for house and garden. (48)

*Numbers in parentheses refer to pages where plant is pictured.

BOTANICAL NAME	COMMON NAME	DESCRIPTION	LIGHT NEEDS	WATER NEEDS	COMMENTS*
Nicodemia diversifolia	Indoor oak	Spreading, arching growth. Bright green leaves lobed like some oaks.	Low or indirect	Moist	Naturally spreading, can be trained as upright plant. (43)
Oncidium sphacelatum		Upright. Yellow flowers spotted or striped with brown.	Indirect	See comments	Water generously during growing season, sparingly during dormant period. (61)
Paphiopedilum	Lady's slipper	Upright, arching growth. Blooms are perky, usually one, occasionally two or more to a stem.	Indirect	Moist	Keep moist at all times. Thrives in less light than most orchids. (11, 30, 49)
Pelargonium domesticum	Lady Washington pelargonium Martha Washington geranium	Upright or somewhat spreading. Leaves heart shaped to kidney shaped, dark green. Large showy flowers 2″ or more across in loose rounded clusters in white and many shades of pink, red, lavender, purple.	Sun or indirect	Dry	Remove faded geranium flowers regularly to encourage new growth. Pinch growing tips in early growth stages to force side branches. Blooms best when somewhat pot-bound. (30, 50)
Pelargonium peltatum	Ivy geranium	Trailing. Leaves rather succulent, glossy, bright green, 2–3″ across, ivylike, with pointed lobes. Single or double flowers in rounded clusters are white, pink, rose, red, and lavender.	Sun or indirect	Dry	Remove faded geranium flowers regularly to encourage new growth. Pinch growing tips in early growth stages to force side branches. Blooms best when somewhat pot-bound. Repot when necessary but only in next larger pot. (47)
Pellaea rotundifolia	Roundleaf fern	Spreading growth. Small fern with fronds up to 1′ long. Nearly round leaflets are evenly spaced and about ¾″ across.	Indirect	Moist to wet	Pretty fern to contrast with finer-textured ferns or to show off in pots or baskets.
Phalaenopsis	Moth orchid	Upright, arching growth. Thick, broad, leathery leaves. Long sprays of 3–6″-wide white, pale yellow, or light lavender or pink flowers from spring through fall.	Indirect	Moist	Require warmer growing conditions than most orchids (minimum 60°–70° F/15°–21° C at night, 70°–85° F/21°–29° C daytime), fairly high humidity, and moist potting medium at all times. (53)
Philodendron selloum		Treelike. 6–8′ or higher, and as wide. Leaves to 3′ long, deeply cut.	Indirect	Moist	Hardiest of big-leafed philodendrons used indoors. (4–5)
Phoenix roebelenii	Pigmy date palm	Tree. Fine-leafed, small-scale palm. One stem grows slowly to 6′ or so. Curved leaves from dense crown.	Indirect	Moist	Excellent pot plant, native to Laos. (8)
Pilea nummulariifolia	Creeping Charlie (one of several plants so named)	Spreading or trailing growth. Leaves rounded and evenly scalloped around edges. Inconspicuous flowers.	Indirect	Dry	Good hanger. Use porous soil mix (1 part sand, 1 part leaf mold, 1 part peat moss). Fertilize monthly with house plant fertilizer. (59)
Platycerium bifurcatum	Staghorn fern	Arching, drooping growth. Odd ferns from tropical regions. Fertile fronds are forked and clustered, gray green, up to 3′ long.	Indirect	Dry	In nature, they grow on trees; gardeners grow them on slabs of bark or tree fern stem, occasionally in hanging baskets or on trees. (30)
Plectranthus	Swedish ivy	Spreading or trailing growth. Leaves somewhat thickish, with scalloped edges and prominent veins. Small white or bluish flowers in spikes.	Indirect or low	Moist to dry	Among easiest plants to grow. Especially good in hanging pot or wall container.
Polyscias fruticosa 'Elegans'	Ming aralia	Shrub. Leaves are finely divided and redivided into multitude of narrow, toothed segments. 'Elegans' is a compact variety with finely cut, dense foliage.	Indirect	Dry	Considered fussy as a house plant; needs fresh air but no drafts, good light but not direct strong sunlight, and just enough water. (37)
Polystichum polyblepharum	Japanese lace fern	Upright, arching growth. Handsome, dense, lacy. Fronds up to 2′.	Low	Moist	Likes standard potting mix with added humus, shade, ample water, average indoor temperatures. (30)
Pteris cretica 'Wimsettii'		Upright, arching growth. Light green fern with forked tips on mature plants.	Indirect or low	Moist	Likes humidity. Excellent table or pedestal display. (30)